THE ENCORE YEARS

ISBN: 979-8-218-93591-7

Cover and interior design by sheerbookdesign.com

THE ENCORE YEARS

Reclaiming Purpose and Visibility
In Your Third Act

RICHARD A. GIAQUINTO

DEDICATION

I dedicate this book to my beautiful wife, Selvi, and to my dear parents; my caring and loving sister, JoAnn; my daughters, Dita and Dyah; the Natawidjaja family; Dave and Natalie; Hope, John, and Priscilla; and Christian, my expert trainer at Equinox.

I also dedicate it to the wonderful people at The Stephen A. Schwarzman Library Building – Marian Gianni, Toisha Tucker, Maeve Bradley, and Geraldine Araujo – for their everyday smiles and kindness, and to all the coaches at the Equinox Gym for their encouragement and good cheer – finally, Yasmine from Amy's Bread for her kindness, support, and coffee and finally, Scarlett for her daily kind words.

Finally, I acknowledge the creative and supportive guidance of my editor, Yen-Yen Lu. Without her insight and dedication, this book would not have been completed.

ACKNOWLEDGMENTS

I am deeply grateful to all the people whose encouragement, support, and inspiration made *The Encore Years* possible.

My heartfelt thanks go to my beautiful wife, Selvi, whose love, patience, and faith sustained me throughout this long journey. I thank my dear parents and my caring and loving sister JoAnn, whose support has guided me through every chapter of my life. To my daughters, Dita and Dyah, your strength, humor, and creativity remind me daily of why I wrote this book.

I also wish to thank my editor, Yen-Yen Lu, whose keen insight, creative guidance, and dedication gave these pages shape and polish.

I also wish to thank Megan Sheer, my book designer and formatter, whose thoughtful design sensibility, patience, and attention to detail brought *The Encore Years* to life on the page.

Special appreciation goes to the excellent staff at The Stephen A. Schwarzman Library Building – Marian Gianni, Toisha Tucker, Maeve Bradley, and Geraldine Araujo – for their smiles, professionalism, and everyday kindness that made writing there such a joy.

I am grateful as well to Christian, my excellent trainer at Equinox Gym, and to all the coaches there whose encouragement kept me energized through the writing process.

Finally, I wish to thank my extended family and friends – the Natawidjajas, Dave, Natalie, and Drs. Holbrook and Finkel, and so many others – for their enthusiasm, friendship, and belief in this project. And to every reader who finds purpose, joy, and renewal in their own encore years– you are the inspiration behind this work.

With respect and kindness,
Richard Anthony Giaquinto

CONTENTS

CHAPTER 1

A HISTORY OF AGEISM

I stopped working full-time two years ago. Fortunately, I had prepared for life after work by reading many books and articles about what experts call the 'encore years'. They highlighted the importance of older adults finding and pursuing their passions after working.

The next day, I unpacked my Gretsch guitar from our basement storage bin. I hadn't played it seriously for ten years. After dusting it off, I attempted a few chords. My fingers felt clumsy and unresponsive. *Shit, what was I thinking?*

I needed advice from respected musicians. Nope, I didn't make any phone calls. Instead, I opened Apple music on my phone and listened to the Beatles, the Rolling Stones, and Animals' classic rock songs. After tapping my foot for just a few minutes, I had my answer. I signed up for lessons at the local music school the following day.

I was initially assigned to a teacher who taught jazz, and I lasted for two short lessons. I had nothing against jazz but I wanted to *rock*, so I requested a teacher who specialized in it. The headteacher made the change. I knew I had made the right choice when I met Patrick in our first lesson. He was a rocker from the heavy metal past. He wore black pants, a dark t-shirt, sneakers with a skeleton pattern, and a black beanie hat over his long blonde hair.

Our first lessons reviewed basic chords, essential scales, and tablature music notation. I also learned simple versions of Beatles songs: 'All My Loving' and 'Hey Jude'. Even more impressive, I soloed while he accompanied me. Yep, I had entered the rock world.

Several months later, I played Paul Simon's song 'Crazy After All These Years' during a lesson. After I finished, Patrick looked at me right in the eyes, smiled, and said, "Rich, that's cool! You nailed it."

"You think so?"

"Yeah. I liked your voice, too."

"Thanks, Patrick."

Patrick opened up his iPad. He looked up and turned to me. "Rich, we have a school recital in January. I want you to perform that song. What do you think?"

I looked at the floor and closed my eyes. "I don't..."

"Rich, it will be good for your playing. We can work together on it."

"I haven't played in front of people since I was 15," I placed my right hand under my chin and imagined myself standing on a stage, sweating. After searching for an excuse, I mumbled, "I'll do it. But you gotta help me. I know I will be terrified."

"Of course, Rich!"

Patrick kept his word. He provided a large font version of the lyrics with the music, and we rehearsed the song during our lessons. I practiced it every night. My wife started singing along with me. I believe my prolonged practice sessions drove her crazy. But she understood my purpose and didn't kill me.

The night of the concert finally arrived, and I spent the day bracing myself for the worst. My biggest fear was sweating so profusely that I would drop the pick and forget the lyrics.

I arrived thirty minutes early and heard other performers. They performed classic rock songs that were released before they were born. It was incredible to watch a fourteen-year-old play Jimi Hendrix's riffs.

Patrick helped me tune my guitar and invited me to sit backstage. I sat down until the announcer said, "Our next performer is Richard Giaquinto, who will perform Paul Simon's 'Still Crazy After All These Years.'"

I snapped to attention and dropped my sheet music to the floor. As I bent down to pick it up, a bright white stage light illuminated me and my bald head. Immediately, I tried to stand and wave. Instead, my legs stiffened, and I lost my balance. I was lucky that a fellow student beside me grabbed my back and kindly guided me to my chair.

I thanked her and raced to the stage. Once I reached the steps, I noticed there was no handrail to help me climb them. More importantly, I needed to find out where Patrick had placed my guitar. I looked around as the stage light followed my every move. It was good that the light didn't pick up on my shaky legs or wide-open mouth trying to scream for help.

"Hey, Rich. Let me help you up the stairs," said Pam, the school's vocal teacher. She held my right arm, guided me up the five steps, and carefully helped me sit in a hard-back chair.

Patrick then climbed the stairs and handed me my guitar. After he plugged me into an amp, he helped me tune it and left. The audience, fearing an impending disaster, remained silent.

My guitar rested on my lap. It felt like a 100-pound weight pushing my body through the stage's wooden floor. I heard footsteps coming up the stairs, and Patrick held his guitar. Within seconds, he sat beside me and said, "Let's do it. 1, 2, 3, 4..."

My clammy hands and trembling left hand reached for my pick. And without thinking, just feeling the powerful, relatable lyrics, I played and sang. "I met my old lover..."

Occasionally, I looked up at the audience. *They're listening to my lousy singing.* As I sang the last verse, "...that life is like a fleeting dream that will fade," the audience nodded in agreement.

The moment we played the last chord, the audience stood and applauded. Patrick had to help me put my guitar on a nearby rack and then help me stand. "Thanks. Thanks. We appreciate it."

Pam appeared immediately and helped me to my seat. People approached me, patted me on the back as I sat, and expressed how much they enjoyed the performance.

After the show, a young guy approached me as I packed up my guitar. "You were great, Richard," he said. "I can't believe you can still play that way. How old are you?"

My heart sunk but I tried to keep a neutral expression as I responded. "Thank you. I'm glad you enjoyed it."

My wife overheard the exchange. She quickly grabbed my arm and pulled me away. She looked at me and whispered, "It's okay, honey. Go to the bathroom and wash up."

I rushed to the bathroom and closed the door behind me. I went to the mirror. My face had turned red, and my hands tightly held onto the bathroom sink. "That guy just unconsciously put me down," I heard myself say. After washing my face with cold water, we left the school for a quiet dinner.

While my performance was successful, there was one drawback. Do you know where it occurred?

You are correct if you guessed my interaction with the young guy. He intended his comment about my playing to be positive. Instead, it came across as passive-aggressive and facetious. Let's examine why.

The dude saw my grey hair, wrinkled face, and inability to climb stairs as symbols of decline and infirmity. He assumed my guitar-playing had suffered the same fate. And when he heard me, it literally blew his mind. I'm sure you experienced the same reaction when you engaged in something you are passionate about. Painting? Gardening? Running? Playing chess?

Applewhite, a writer and activist for the rights of older adults, refers to this stereotyping as ageism. She explains that ageism occurs when a person unfairly judges or mistreats another individual based on age. Certain ageist beliefs about older adults are taught to us from the time that we are children. We accept them without resistance; they become how we view older adults for the rest of our lives. [1,2]

Applewhite refers to this surprised reaction to an older adult's ability to perform a task supposedly out of their reach as 'inspiration porn'. [1] I believe that it is demeaning and emphasizes age instead of celebrating the accomplishment.

Applewhite believes the cause of this reaction stems from society's role in developing a belief system concerning aging. It follows these two formulas:

Youth = Good + Contributing + Purpose

Old = Bad + Decline + Lost

Therefore, when an unsuspecting person witnesses an older adult doing something as 'impressive' as playing guitar and singing, it shatters their belief system. They then speak to the older adult to understand this unexpected rarity and ease their confusion. [1]

I wrote this book for people like me who have entered what others have called our 'encore years'. These are the years immediately after we stop working. Now that we have more time, we must make choices that ensure a productive and enjoyable new life filled with meaning and purpose. This book provides guidance, suggestions, and information to help you transition from a work-centered life to one focused on pursuing your dreams and discovering a new purpose.

A HISTORY OF AGEISM

1860-1914

The the traditional age hierarchy changed significantly with industrialization (1860-1914), which led to a shift toward urbanization. The youth regarded industrialization as an opportunity for improved living. They left their family farms, while the older generation stayed behind and fulfilled their traditional roles. [2]

Losing the younger generation at farms or rural communities devastated multi-generational families. As a result, the older adults lost their in-home support system. Local authorities and local houses of worship stepped in to provide the missing guidance and help. Despite their charitable actions, the community shunned and marginalized them. [2]

During America's colonial times, from the early 1600s until the mid-1700s, society considered older adults essential and productive members. In fact, experienced farmers led their communities and taught future farmers. [2]

Factory owners required older adults who left their farms to work as hard as their younger counterparts. If they couldn't meet these work standards, management fired them. Historians note that this was the first instance of workplace discrimination. Some returned to farming, while others remained in these industrial cities. Those who remained and were unemployed presented a problem for the local governments – feeding, clothing, and housing.[2]

Local politicians and businesses responded in two distinct ways. First, they provided pensions to older workers forced out of their jobs. Second, to help manage their business finances and accounting practices, they invented a new word to describe the non-working period: 'retirement'. After a while, as more older workers entered retirement, the government and media began portraying retirement as a time of withdrawal and decline.

As the number of retirees increased, the working public saw retirees as a burden on society – useless, frail, and unproductive. The hostility and hatred towards this select group led to ageism – the unfair treatment of individuals based on their age.[1,2]

Widows and unmarried older women living in cities suffered the same humiliation. Since they could not work and support themselves, local governments forced them to live in asylums and poorhouses.[2]

Segregating and labeling this demographic changed public perception of older people, making them seem feeble and unproductive. This notion of the adverse effects of aging has led people to fear and hate the idea of getting older.[2]

TWENTIETH AND TWENTY-FIRST CENTURIES

Pensions first appeared after the Civil War. The Government provided financial help to disabled veterans, surviving widows, and their children. The American Express Company (1875) provided workers with pension funds when they turned sixty and had an excellent record. [2] In 1935, the US Government passed the Social Security Act in response to the Great Depression. The law established that workers should retire at sixty-five or older and receive funds to ensure a comfortable life in their remaining years. Furthermore, to ensure that older adults contribute to their pension, the Internal Revenue Service established an exemption for workers who put money into their pensions. [2] Sadly, these government actions had unintended outcomes. They created an unfavorable and negative opinion of retirees. Yes, older adults had access to financial help – however, the public labeled them as infirm, senile, incapacitated, and obsolete. Unfortunately, these prejudices from the 1930s created a foundation for ageist beliefs that still exist in our society today. [1,2]

In the 1960s, the Civil Rights movement drew attention to the evils of discriminating and segregating older adults. Organizations and government laws tried to prevent age discrimination in the workplace and the most important law occurred in 1967. The Congress enacted the Age Discrimination Act (ADEA) to protect older workers' rights. Many employers advertised job openings with age restriction, such as 'no one over

35 should apply' or specifying an age range, for example, 21 to 35. Later. Congress strengthened the ADEA by removing all age limits for employment.

A CHANCE TO MAKE MONEY

In the 1950s, entrepreneurs smelled the opportunity to make money, and 'activity theory' was one way to do so. Let me explain.

Entrepreneurs, especially in Florida and Arizona, read and re-read this theory. They especially liked the idea of 'community'. After receiving funds from investors, they purchased land and constructed self-contained communities for active retirees. [2]

The ads promised a permanent vacation and a chance to live in a new community far from the life they left behind. It worked. Older adults flocked to these places of paradise. This societal shift, influenced by ageist perceptions, led to the creation of retirement communities. Sadly, society and the media convinced them they were no longer contributing members of their own communities. So, they sold their homes, left their families, and settled in these 'active' communities.

During this same period, research shows that other older adults preferred to remain in their homes and communities while transitioning to life without work. To ensure a safe and high quality of life, they invested additional funds in installing stair lift chairs, walk-in showers, increased lighting, and computer-based applications that support medical devices and control home appliances.

The most important outcome of the period for older adults was that society allowed them to decide where to spend the rest of their lives. This victory would later help older adults try to redefine what it means to be retired.

MY ENCORE YEARS

My wife often tells her colleagues and friends that I'm living a version of *Golden Years*, one of her favorite TV shows, because I have a fulfilling life and have reinvented who I am. Luckily, I have my health and have been able to develop meaningful, purpose-driven encore years.

Since retiring, I self-published my memoir and I am now working on my second book – this book. I train in the gym six times a week with the guidance of a trainer for two of these sessions. I returned to my first passion: music. I started guitar lessons again and currently play in a rock band. Finally, and most importantly, I married for the first time at 72 – the best thing I have ever done.

While forming these new habits was difficult, I drew upon the emotional and cognitive skills I developed throughout my life. There were a few missteps along the way, but when this happened, I took a step back to reassess and make adjustments – just as I used to do throughout my career. I am confident if you use those skills in your encore years, and you will also succeed.

CHAPTER 2

LIFE AFTER WORK: THE ENCORE YEARS

They just see grey hair, and they write you off.

Arynita Armstrong

I had a fifty-year career as an educator in New York City; the first thirty as a teacher and administrator. It was a challenging yet rewarding experience.

For the last twenty years, I have worked as a professor at a local college. It was my dream job. I taught first-generation college students who wanted to teach in our local schools. They worked hard, laughed at my crummy jokes, and always amazed me with their intelligence and interest in making a difference in some kid's life.

But as the years went by, I realized my energy and stamina could no longer meet the demands of a dedicated professor. So, at the end of the spring semester 2019, I retired. I remember when I told my graduating class; we openly cried together. It is something I will never forget.

Initially, I was hesitant about having a retirement party. I knew it would be an emotional affair and I wasn't sure if I was ready. However, my colleagues, who had become my friends over the years, convinced me it was a necessary celebration of my career.

The Committee used the former meeting hall as the venue. It was a spacious room with carpeted floors, high ceilings, and bay windows that let in the warm spring sunlight. It reminded me of my parents' living room on many Easter Sundays as we eagerly awaited our guests.

I was nervous as hell. Because it was the end of the semester, I didn't expect many people to attend. However, as the Dean led me into the room, I noticed it was crowded.

As I sat next to my colleague, I looked around the room. I was happy to see Paula, a philosophy professor, and Dave, who taught mathematics; they expressed kind words about how much the school would miss me. Unfortunately, Andrew, a pretentious English lecturer, sat at the next table. After a few minutes, he shook my hand, explaining he had to leave because of a previous commitment. I thanked God when Janice, my department colleague, approached the podium.

Janice presented a PowerPoint presentation about my time at the college. She highlighted my teaching classes, observing student teachers, leading clubs, and closed with five slides emphasizing my students laughing at my attempts at humor. I remembered that my jokes eased the tension in my classroom. Most of my students worked part-time while carrying a full course load. So, during my class, especially after an hour, I would tell a joke or relate a personal story about my days as a teacher or my crazy childhood days in my Italian Brooklyn neighborhood. After we laughed together, I would resume the class topic. Seeing the final five slides brought tears to my eyes, making it hard to conceal my emotions.

It made me realize that I had lost sight of my contributions to my college as a professor. Linda, who sat beside me, noticed my tearful reaction and quietly offered me some tissues. I lowered my head and wiped the tears away.

The next day, I sat on my easy chair and realized I no longer had a job. My thinking could be summed up with this troubling thought: "Shit, what do I do now?"

I had read several books about preparing for retirement, but the suggestions about moving to and living in an enclosed gated community did not appeal to me. I wanted to maintain my independence and live in my apartment with my wife.

My teaching career had defined who I was for much of my life. I became a teacher and taught in schools in economically disadvantaged areas because I faced similar obstacles in my youth and wanted to help others overcome them. The thirty years I spent in these schools challenged my beliefs and stamina, but the rewards far outnumbered the setbacks I faced.

As a college professor, I had a similar experience. My students needed more than a simple education. They needed direction, a role model, and someone to listen to them. We shared our cultural background and values. I often spoke about family expectations and the pressures to succeed. I felt needed and appreciated.

I used my office hours to help students select the correct classes, answer questions about assignments, and discuss reasons for grades. Occasionally, we also discuss stress-related issues, career choices, and matters of family or friendship. I did my best in demonstrating the qualities of a caring teacher who respects, listens, and is fair. Since they were teachers-in-training, this approach was essential to their development.

True, I had affected and changed many lives. But I had neglected my own. Now, I had to shift gears and think about what was best for me.

I spent the summer traveling in Italy. I spent three weeks in Florence, hoping to find answers. A concierge suggested I apply for library use at the National Central Library of Florence (*Biblioteca Oblate*). Within hours, I was sitting in a historic room with vaulted ceiling with religious-themed frescoes. Miniature paintings of various religious virtues of hope and charity hung on the walls and stained-glass windows filled the space with soft light, creating a perfect for studying and writing.

I started to free-write – a creative writing technique where a person writes for a set time without worrying about grammar, a unified theme, or writing structure. Strangely, my ideas centered on memories from my childhood in Brooklyn. After reliving these amusing memories, I jotted down my concerns about retirement. I remember these particular words:

- Empty

- Scared

- Boring

- Lost

- Anxious

I needed air and headed for the *Piazza Della Signoria*. An espresso and cannoli at *Café Rivoire would* be my reward. I needed time and food to help me confront and accept the prospect that I might soon retire. Two days later, I was home. I started to read *The New York Times*, something I had not been able to enjoy while working. One Sunday morning, I found an article by the author Marc Freedman. In the article, he explained that retirement should be more than just a time for leisure but a time for pursuing 'meaningful activities'.

He compared this period of freedom to an *encore* that a performer takes after a brilliant performance. He emphasized that retirement is not a withdrawal but a time for rediscovery. A gift, a chance to redefine who you are. To learn a new language, travel the world, or even the opportunity to pursue a lifelong passion – painting, playing guitar, and gardening. It's your second chance, an encore, where you can finally escape the confines of working full-time and raising a family.

The concept of 'encore years' got me thinking. I did more reading and self-reflection and realized I had to choose between two paths. My first option was for my wife and I to move to a private gated retirement community where a paid staff would cater to all our daily needs. This lifestyle would allow us to relax and enjoy planned activities with others. While this choice offered benefits, it would probably result in a substantial loss of personal autonomy.

The second approach we considered was to embrace the concept of the 'encore years' fully. This choice would allow us to stay in our apartment, make our own choices about living, and maintain control over our lives.

I think you guessed I chose the latter. You would be correct. Believe me, I have nothing against that choice to live in a retirement community. It's not for me. As long as I was healthy, I wanted to pursue activities I couldn't do while working full-time. I refer to them as the Big Five:

- Writing and reading

- Playing rock guitar

- Exercising consistently

- Traveling

- Watching movies

I have now concluded my fourth encore year, or some folks call the Third Act, and at 76, I am doing okay.[3] Luckily, I still have my health and can still use New York City's public transportation to travel as needed. Here are some of my accomplishments from my Encore Years:

- I got married at age 72

- I published my first book at age 75 and I am now working on my second

- I played in a rock band once a week and participated in five music concerts

- I became a gym fanatic and boxed with a trainer twice a week

It wasn't easy. I have had my share of bad days. But I have a secret weapon. You have it, too. It is the accumulated emotional, cognitive, and practical experience over our working years. For instance, addressing workplace conflict, managing personal or professional disappointment, or balancing work and private life. Whenever there is a semblance of doubt or inner conflict, I call upon this reserve and, in most cases, overcome any problem or resistance.

It's crucial that you are satisfied with your selection. It should align with your lifestyle and current physical and mental well-being. If you have any illnesses or mobility challenges, a retirement community may be your best option. However, if you are relatively healthy and can move around freely, staying in your home is a sensible choice. However, these are not hard and fast rules. Whatever decision you make, it should satisfy your emotional and physical needs.

CHAPTER 3

MEDICINE AND AGING

What do you expect at your age?

Ashton Applewhite

I have played guitar for over 50 years since my teenage years, only taking occasional breaks for school, career, and family responsibilities. Throughout those years, I learned the importance of practice for a musician. Even as a more experienced musician, I continue practicing and rehearsing before performing.

When I finish playing a show, the audience rewards my efforts with loud applause. I accept that as a sign of respect, as do my fellow musicians.

After the show, I found a vacant room. I leaned my guitar against the wall. It appeared as tired as I was. As an introvert, getting on the stage and performing turned me inside out. My body and brain felt empty. I used all my energy up and felt weightless. It was a good thing I was alone so I could re-energize. But there was something I needed to remember. *You played a show and received applause. I'm proud of you, Richard. Take another bow for yourself.* I stood up, faced the mirror on the wall, and bowed like Eric Clapton.

I knew that my wife and daughters were waiting for me outside. So, I took a quiet breath, opened the door, and headed to the refreshment area.

My wife and I went to get some coffee together. "Honey, you sounded great," she said. "Even though I heard that song a hundred times at home, it moved me. I finally understand why you like it so much."

I kissed her and realized my left hand had finally stopped shaking. After my second cup of coffee, a guy wearing a Led Zeppelin t-shirt, wide-legged jeans, and long, curly hair came up to me and said, "Hey, that was awesome. I dug your solo. MAN! How old are you, dude?"

Ashton Applewhite, in her book *This Chair Rocks*, classifies this response as a particular form of Ageism called 'inspiration porn'. She explains that the reaction comes from disbelief that older adults can perform activities attributed to younger people. [1]

Why this reaction? Society and our culture have taught younger people that older adults are frail, declining in health, and lifeless. This teaching begins in childhood and continues for the rest of their lives. Interestingly, they will experience the same responses when they are older adults.

I hate to admit that when I perform, I often receive these responses marked by disbelief regarding my ability to still play at my age. I select complex songs, ranging from Jimi Hendrix to the Beatles.

My usual response to this reaction: "Thanks so much. I take lessons and practice daily." I ignore their question about my age. For me, it's not a relevant factor.

AGEISM IN MEDICINE

In her excellent book *Breaking the Code*, Becca Levy suggests that the medical profession often treats aging as a disease. Levy identifies five areas where this occurs: [1,6]

1. *Overprescribing medications* occurs when doctors misdiagnose standard signs of aging (backache, fatigue, or stiff joints) as medical conditions and prescribe multiple medications that might interact with and cause harmful drug interactions or side effects. Levy points out that the pharmaceutical industry supports these treatments not because they help older adults but because they add to their profit margin.

2. *On the other hand, doctors may also dismiss symptoms* as part of the aging process. A comment that many older adults might hear is: "What do you expect at your age?" This misdiagnosis of pain, fatigue, or forgetfulness because of someone's age might neglect the treatment of a complex medical issue. [5,6]

3. *The use of aggressive interventions via cosmetic surgery* (such as facelifts, eyelid surgery, or neck lifts) to halt or reverse age-related changes often have a limited effect on someone's quality of life. Levy attributes this reliance on these procedures to society's belief that aging signifies decline and loss of interest in meaningful life. Society has subjected older adults to this message since childhood, and the media – both traditional and social media – bombard us continually with commercials suggesting a cure for this *'disease'.* Sensing

a way to profit from this perception, the beauty industry, the complicit media, and the medical profession developed over the years, products, services, and expensive medical procedures to address this perceived need. They realized that "There's money in grey." [4, 6]

4. Preventive care for treatable conditions in older adults, such as depression, osteoporosis, and arthritis, is often overlooked as these conditions are frequently viewed as a 'normal part of aging'. As a result, medical practitioners mistakenly believe that treatment may be ineffective. [1, 3, 6]

5. *Lastly, medical professionals often use a one-size-fits-all approach* because they view older adults as a homogenous group. This neglects the fact that they are individuals with different health needs, lifestyles, or interests. This oversight can lead to generalized care, a lack of respect for the person, or a misdiagnosis. [4-6]

Levy also criticizes the media for promoting the belief that aging is a disease and a time of decline. For example, I watch news shows on network television and cable. Most commercials feature medications older adults use: Humira for autoimmune diseases, Eliquis to prevent strokes, and Lyrica to lessen nerve pain.

When I see these commercials, I dislike how the commercials portray older adults as frail, in decline, and dependent. Sometimes, I worry I might develop the disease depicted, and it makes me feel anxious. Lastly, if I had the disease, could I afford its cost?

As older adults, we fall victim to this manipulation. These pharmaceutical commercials know older adults are prone to heart disease, cancer, respiratory illnesses, stroke, and Alzheimer's disease. They prey on our fears, but it only benefits the networks profiting from broadcasting these stylized advertisements. [3]

EXAMPLES OF AGEISM IN MEDICINE

Healthcare providers treating older adults view symptoms like balance issues, incontinence, or constipation as normal parts of aging and believe they are not treatable. This inconclusive diagnosis leaves the older adult without the necessary medication. The geriatrician Mark Lachs writes about this reliance on age for a medical diagnosis in his book *Treat Me, Not My Age*, an apt title that perfectly sums up this medical negligence. [5]

In the book, he calls for a more personalized and non-ageist approach to medicine. He sums up the approach the medical establishment has for aged patients in this definitive quote: "Medical ageism often results in a patient's ailments going untreated or being overtreated because their symptoms are dismissed as 'just part of getting older.'" [5]

In his book, Dr. Lachs challenges this viewpoint and offers practical advice to counter ageist beliefs. He warns that older adults frequently face misdiagnosis, overmedication, and dismissed treatable conditions such as depression and insomnia. He suggests taking control of your medical care by having a solid plan and being persistent. Here are his recommended steps to prepare for a doctor's appointment: [5]

- Take the lead. Organize your thoughts and prioritize your concerns. If something doesn't feel right physically or emotionally, get it checked out.

- Prepare for your doctor's visit like you would a business meeting. Know the purpose of the visit, describe your present medical condition, familiarize yourself with your family's history, and remind yourself that you are in control of the situation.

- Bring a list of medications and keep an ongoing record of vital health numbers, such as blood pressure, cholesterol, triglycerides, blood glucose, and thyroid function levels. It is helpful to provide facts and evidence to support your case.

- Clearly state your main complaint. Ask questions and request clarifications when necessary. Take notes and make sure to have a specific follow-up plan. Don't be overwhelmed just because you are in the presence of a doctor.

- Request visuals to help you better understand your medical situation. For example, digital imaging, charts, models of body parts, and illustrated brochures and pamphlets.

- If healthcare providers use patronizing language during your visit, assert yourself as someone with a lifetime of knowledge and intelligence.

The medical establishment of ageist practices with older women is also unacceptable. Applewhiteand Levy identified the following disparities in the medical treatment of women: [1,6]

- Older women are less likely to speak up about their health condition in a medical setting because they fear medical providers will identify them as complainers.

- They experience more waiting time for a final diagnosis than men.

- Doctors often minimize their health concerns and attribute them to just getting old.

- Medical practitioners often disregard specific ailments, pain, and fatigue, diagnosing them as psychological rather than physical.

- Women may fear the final diagnosis because of potential hospitalization and loss of independence.

- Women fear their doctors will rush their visits and ignore their medical concerns.

- There may be some embarrassment around their lack of understanding of medical terminology during the visits.

- Older women may lack of funds to pay for any required medical care.

Women are underrepresented in clinical trials for leading diseases – Harvard Medical School reported this in 2022:

- Cardiovascular disease: women make-up 49% of patients diagnosed with this disease; in clinical trials, only 41.9% of participants were women.

- Psychiatric Disorders: women make-up 60% of patients diagnosed with this disease; in clinical trials, only 42% of participants were women.

- Cancer: women make-up 51% of patients diagnosed with this disease; in clinical trials, only 41% of participants were women.

Doctors spend less time and use limited patient-centered communication with older adults, resulting in limited involvement in decisions about proper treatment and care. [1,6] Moreover, research on illnesses often excludes the participation of older adults in the National Institutes of Health. [1,6]

Finally, and most problematically, most residents decline the opportunity to specialize in geriatric medicine. They regard it as a low-paying and less prestigious field than others.

Furthermore, treating younger patients is more challenging because it is faster, easier, more profitable, and less emotionally draining.

The discussion above appears overly pessimistic. However, we have made progress in lessening the trend of ageism in medicine. [1,6]

BECCA LEVY

In Becca Levy *Breaking the Age Code*, she suggests a three-stage model for confronting ageism which can be applied to various scenarios within a healthcare setting. [6]

- Raise awareness about ageism by exposing it when you see it, hear it, or witness it.

- Place the blame of ageism on its source and call out the individuals using it.

- Advocate for ourselves – get involved in politics, call out ageist content in media – both visual and print – and speak to other people, such as friends and family, about your experiences with ageism.

EXERCISE

Read the scene and answer the questions below. Answers are provided at the end of this section.

Scene 1: *Immediate Care Center's examining room.*

Characters: Jennifer Orlando, a retired firefighter, age 67, Dr. Liz Chandler, age 40, and Nurse Hector Palto, age 32.

NURSE HECTOR: (speaking slowly and loudly) Good morning! I need to weigh you and take your blood pressure.

JENNIFER: (stares at him) Okay.

She climbs on the scale and Hector offers her his hand. She pushes it away. He notes down her weight and then takes her blood pressure.

NURSE HECTOR: 120 over 80 – your blood pressure is excellent!

JENNIFER: That's great. I try to run at least three miles each day by the East River but –

She is interrupted as DR. LIZ CHANDLER walks in carrying a folder.

DR. LIZ CHANDLER: Hello, Ms. Orlando. I'm Dr. Liz Chandler. How can I help you today?

JENNIFER: My left knee is bothering me. I haven't been able to run lately and I really miss it. Can you look at it and see what's wrong?

DR. LIZ CHANDLER: (glancing down at her folder) It says here that you're 67 – wow! You don't look your age at all.

NURSE HECTOR: (still speaking loudly and slowly) And she says she runs three miles every day! Amazing, right?

Jennifer smiles but looks uncomfortable.

DR. LIZ CHANDLER: (condescending) Well, perhaps it may be getting harder to run regularly. You should be taking it easy at your age! But if you are concerned, we can take an X-ray to ease any worries you might have.

NURSE HECTOR: (loud whisper, to Liz) Otherwise they will just keep pestering you for an answer as usual.

They smirk at each other. Jennifer notices but doesn't comment.

JENNIFER: Thank you, doctor.

Scene 2: 30 minutes later, in Dr. Chandler's office. Jennifer sits in a comfortable chair. Dr. Chandler is looking at the X-ray on her laptop. She appears puzzled and types something on her keyboard.

DR. CHANDLER: I am sorry for keeping you waiting. Thank you for your patience. (*She glances at her laptop screen again*) You said you run three miles every day? Is that right?

JENNIFER: Yes. I have been running for over 20 years now.

DR. CHANDLER: That's amazing! (*sighs*) Unfortunately, I have some bad news for you. You have a condition known as runner's knee caused by poor running form. It usually happens to younger runners which is why… (*she trails off*)

JENNIFER: (*shocked*) Well, how do you treat it? Will I ever be able to run again?

DR. CHANDLER: (*brisk, professional, reassuring*) Look, you'll have plenty of options. I will arrange a physical therapy appointment at the local sports injury center and we'll go from there. You may have to attend regular sessions there for a while, but many people are able to heal. According to Nurse Hector's assessment, you are in very good health. I'm sure you'll be able to return to running in no time.

JENNIFER: *(relieved)* Thank you, doctor.

QUESTIONS:

1. What are the examples of ageism here?

2. Who is to blame for its use?

3. Who should we call/out and challenge?

ANSWERS:

1. The examples of ageism begin with Hector assuming he has to speak slowly (elder speak) because Jennifer is an older adult. He also assumed that she needed help to get off the scale and was amazed by how easily she did so. In addition, Dr. Chandler initially believed Jennifer's age was the cause of her knee issue.

2. Society and medical training are to blame for conditioning Dr. Chandler and Hector to believe that older adults are in a state of decline, fragility, and lack enthusiasm for continued exercise.

3. We have to call out Dr. Chandler and Hector, but we can do it conversationally. For example, Jennifer could have responded this way:

- "Hi Hector, thanks for being such a gentleman for trying to help me off the scale but I am capable of doing so myself. I exercise at a gym and concentrate on strengthening my legs and improving my balance. I do these functional exercises so I can maintain my independence. Thanks. Please remember this the next time I'm here."

- "Hi, Dr. Chandler. Thanks for taking the time and effort to diagnose my knee problem. I appreciate your concern and thoroughness. But please remember in the future that older adults have medical issues that might not be because of their age. It might be a medical issue caused by an active lifestyle or something else entirely. Please remember that aging is not a disease."

Ageism unconsciously affects us because we have experienced it so often as older adults. Most of the time, we accept it or ignore it. I am convinced that this must stop.

Without realizing it, being the subject of ageist remarks, no matter how small, affects how we perceive ourselves. Levy suggests that recipients of ageist words develop an unhealthy or damaging view of the aging process. Over time, this leads to depression, isolation, and loss of independence. [6]

We must confront the issue whenever it emerges to preserve our optimistic perspective on aging.

PRACTICAL TIPS TO FIGHT MEDICAL AGEISM AND THE POWER OF YOUNGER GENERATION IN THIS FIGHT [5, 6]

SUGGESTIONS FOR OFFSETTING AGEIST PRACTICES IN MEDICAL CARE:

If, as an older adult, you experience an ageist remark or interaction from a medical provider. I recommend these techniques: [5, 6]

- Recognize and challenge the incident. Use your lifelong experiences with difficult people to confront this ageist behavior. You might say, "Aging brings changes to my body, but I want to discuss all potential causes."

- In your discussion with the doctor, ask about ways to improve your condition beyond medication, including diet changes, exercise, rehabilitation, and preventative care options.

- Consider seeking a geriatrician for this second opinion.

- Speak to peers as a means of support.

YOUNGER PEOPLE TO THE RESCUE

It is also important for younger people to recognize and combat ageism towards older adults. In each event described below, I have listed some suggestions below on how a younger person may call out ageism towards older adults, including rational responses from a younger adult in situations where I received an ageist remark from someone. [5,6]

- They might explain why the comment is not valid and provide evidence. For example, when someone suggests I'm too old to play a song, my teacher responds, "He's played more difficult songs than this. This is nothing new for him."

- They might also try to turn an ageist remark into something positive. At the gym, when some gym rat says, "I can't believe you still work out." My trainer might respond with: "Richard is here six days a week. He inspires me to work out harder."

- They might also challenge a person's expectations of an older adult. As a dedicated writer and participant in a research program at a local public institution, I was interrupted by a fellow writer during lunch with a doctoral candidate. He said, "It's a beautiful spring day. Why are you sitting in a room writing?" and the doctoral candidate responded quickly: "Thank God he's here. I learned so much from him. I'm grateful he is here sharing his expertise with me."

I'd like to end this chapter with a quote from Dr. Mark Lach's book, *What your doctor won't tell you about getting older: An insider's survival manual for outsmarting the healthcare system.* He says: "our mission, should you decide to accept it, is to make sure that medical ageism doesn't undermine your medical care and your health, through undertreatment, overtreatment, or no treatment." I hope this might inspire you to take your health concerns seriously and implore others, particularly in the medical profession, to do the same. [5 (845)]

CHAPTER 4

THE MEDIA AND AGEISM

The media is the message.

Marshall McLuhan

MARGINALIZATION IN THE MEDIA

I have a brainteaser to begin this chapter on the media and ageism. Below, you will find the names of five famous films. The question is: what do these films have in common?[8, 10]

- *Hansel and Gretel* (2013)
- *Dirty Grandpa* (2016)
- *The Bucket List* (2007)
- *Gran Torino* (2008)
- *The Fabulous Four* (2024)
- *Moana* (2016)

ANSWER: The movies negatively portray older adults using ageist stereotypes.

- *Hansel and Gretel:* The witch in the story is depicted as old, ugly, dangerous and untrustworthy. [12]

- *Dirty Grandpa:* This film that depicts an older man (played by Robert De Niro) in degrading ways: rude, trying to regain his youth by chasing younger women, and refusing to adopt the traditional role of a grandfather because it symbolizes a loss of freedom, fun and purpose. [13]

- *The Bucket List:* This film follows two older adults who embark on adventures, such as skydiving, traveling, and racing cars, before they die. While this illustrates strength, it also portrays aging as a loss of time instead of an opportunity to embrace it. [13]

- *Gran Torino:* Clint Eastwood plays a stubborn and angry war veteran who strictly adheres to the values from the previous century. He struggles to adapt and he discriminates against his Asian neighbors. At the end of the film, he sacrifices his life for the good, and his demise makes room for an enlightened younger generation, emphasizing the offensive belief that older generations are disposable.[8]

- *The Fabulous Four* is a film about four lifelong friends who travel to Florida for a friend's wedding. The women, in their late sixties, are portrayed as out of touch, attempting to act young again, longing for love and attention, and making jokes about the effects of aging on their bodies. [16]

- *Moana:* The film portrays Tala as the village crazy, eccentric, and wise. The implied message is that Tala is expendable because of her age and dies so the young Moana can reach her potential and destiny. [12]

Writers Applewhite and Gendron state that the films or the other arts reflect society's view of older adults. Therefore, films portray older adults as infirmed, unproductive, and out of touch. As a result, the movie industry seldom depicts older adults in major roles in nuanced stories involving adventure, love, or personal growth. [1,11]

That being said, I think it is appropriate to discuss films that do make efforts towards a balanced portrayal of older adults in film. [2,23]

- *The Best Exotic Marigold Hotel* (2011): The film takes in India where recent retirees find adventure, new love, and a new sense of purpose. [2,23]

- BBC's *Miss Marple* film series (1984–1992): I love Miss Marple because I see my mom in this brilliant, independent, and dedicated detective. [2,23]

- *It's Complicated:* Meryl Streep's character, Jane, an older adult, is portrayed as an independent, successful woman, who can still be involved in romance – a love triangle. [2,23]

- *A Man Called Otto* (2022): The film features Tom Hanks as a lonely widower who discovers new meaning and purpose in life after forming a friendship with a young family that moves in next door. [2,23]

- *Live Twice, Love Once* (2009): The film beautifully tells a story of a retired professor who has the beginning stages of Alzheimer's who tries to find his long-lost love. It vividly shows that even with the possibility of facing immediate cognitive decline, an older adult can keep his dignity, ability to love, and sense of purpose. [2, 23]

TELEVISION

I will be honest here. Television has made some progress in its portrayal of older adults in more recent years and there have been many shows that I've enjoyed. *A Man on the Inside* stars Ted Danson as an intelligent, purpose-driven older adult, a widower who becomes an undercover detective in a retirement community. The show also features many other older actors – Sally Struthers (*All in the Family*), John Getz (*Blood Simple*), and Lori Tan Chinn (*Roseanne*) – and gives them rich and complex storylines that allow their acting abilities to shine.

Only Murders in the Building features two older characters (played by Steve Martin and Martin Short) teaming up with a younger colleague to solve mysteries together. Martin and Short's characters are depicted as resourceful, clever, and even embracing the use of technology in their work. It also depicts intergenerational friendships as a wonderful way for people from different age groups to learn from each other. Similarly, in the show *Hacks*, Jean Smart plays a successful older comedian who is resilient, adaptive, and perceptive who equally mentors and learns from younger colleagues.

Reality shows are also starting to include older adults and their authentic stories. *The Golden Bachelorette* is a dating game show which follows a dynamic woman in her 60s who is seeking a meaningful relationship with older male contestants, demonstrating that older adults still have the capacity to find love and meaningful connections while allowing themselves to feel vulnerable.

Despite this success, a 2025 AARP survey found that older adults still consider the depiction of their lives as stereotypical and demeaning. They argue that older adults should have more leading roles that reflect their active, fulfilling lives. [6]

One finding I found concerning was that, according to AARP, over half (52%) observed no improvement in the portrayal of older adults over the past five years, while only 28% noted any progress. [6]

On a final note, another statistic from the survey found that older adults collectively spend approximately 10 billion dollars annually on television streaming services. Despite this evidence of consumer spending, the media mentioned above still marginalizes older adults. [6]

DIGITAL PLATFORMS

Instagram, TikTok, and YouTube often depict older adults in stereotypical ways similar to those seen in other media: feeble, in decline, have memory loss, and lack mobility.

The stars of these platforms, influencers, target their messages to a younger audience. These popular and influential individuals promote anti-aging products. Their underlying message is *that aging is to be fought, not accepted.*

The deliberate marginalization of older adults on various media platforms was also apparent during the COVID-19 pandemic. Social media platforms contained inflammatory posts about older adults, referring to them as 'casket fillers' and suggesting that the pandemic was 'boomer removal'. [17]

These remarks are further proof of the poor treatment of older folks in the media. Younger generations need more understanding and appreciation for those who came before them. Because we do not have a virtual presence in the world that they inhabit daily, there is less chance they will see us in an accurate light and sympathize with our needs and interests. [17]

However, older adults have become influencers on these platforms and increased their visibility. I have listened to/watched Dr. Jordan Peterson on YouTube discuss issues involving self-improvement and cultural issues. Helen Van Winkle (also known as Baddie Winkle) is a prominent internet personality who became an Instagram influencer who promotes body positivity and advocates against the evils of ageism in our culture.

Podcasting is also part of the presence of older adults having influence. Julia Louis-Dreyfus has a podcast, *Wiser Than Me,* where she interviews older adults who are older and 'wiser' than her. Lisa Stockdale's podcast, *Aging in Full Bloom,* discusses relevant issues for older adults. Her podcast addresses key topics such as preserving family histories, managing arthritis pain, using technology for successful aging in place, home-delivered nutrition programs, and educating listeners about online fraud and scams.

ADVERTISING

In their ad campaigns, many companies rely on a stereotypical representation of older adults to sell products and make a profit. We have already noted that society views aging as a decline, the end of aspirations and dreams, and something to be feared. Therefore, the media concentrates its efforts on the younger members of society.

Two of the most problematic ad campaigns I have seen recently include Progressive Insurance's 'Parentamorphosis' campaign. These commercials humorously depict new homeowners turning into their parents, highlighting undesirable behaviors associated with older generations. While comedic, some argue they perpetuate negative stereotypes about aging.

One example takes place at a gas station. In this ad, a new homeowner observes a younger man filling his truck with gasoline. He strikes up a conversation by commenting on the young man's dirt bike, reminiscent of the conversations his father might have had years ago. This ageist concept in the ad implies that fathers often engage in unnecessary chatter, particularly with younger people, simply to hear their own voices.

The other commercial comes from Tide and involves a young couple discussing their new heavier load of laundry because of their new household members: grandma and grandpa. The final scene features a bewildered grandpa entering, looking confused and wearing only his underwear as he searches for his pants. Again, this is intended to have humorous effect, but it relies on the harmful idea of older generations being helpless and dependent on younger people.

My research has identified pharmaceutical companies as one of the few institutions that target their campaign ads for older adults and place them as the central focus in their advertising. They recognize that older adults are the primary consumer base for their products because, as people age, they require ongoing medical treatment and medications. This recognition may drive research and innovation, but it is also a significant financial burden for older adults with limited financial resources as well as increasing health anxiety for a vulnerable age group, which I have discussed in a previous chapter. [5,15,21]

THE EFFECTS OF MARGINALIZATION ON OLDER ADULTS

PSYCHOLOGICALLY

Seeing your age group portrayed negatively can result in low self-esteem. Even worse, the lack of aged characters in print and visual media prevents other age groups from understanding and appreciating the value and wisdom of older adults.

BEHAVIORALLY

Low self-esteem causes older adults to develop a fatalistic attitude toward aging. As a result, they may stop taking prescribed medication, refuse to exercise, and stop living a productive, purposeful, and meaningful lifestyle.

The unhappiness caused by this marginalization forces the body to release harmful chemicals – cortisol – into our blood. High levels of these chemicals cause stress, depression, and anxiety. Sadly, persistent emotional problems can lead to an earlier death. [14]

The severe effect of this marginalization has many implications. Since older adults are invisible or depreciated in the media, the problems they confront daily go largely unnoticed by the general public – lack of access to transportation, loneliness, and depression, to name a few. This has a domino effect which reaches larger powers, such as local politicians or national leaders. Consequently, funding is allocated to more visible issues – infrastructure repairs, educational methods, and defense and national security. [1, 6, 10, 11, 16]

While writing this section, I had a flashback to my college days. I remember reading Marshall McLuhan's work on the impact and influence of the media on how we think, communicate, and understand our reality.

I recall a particular instance during my graduate studies, when John Lennon went from being a beloved Beatle to facing criticism for his anti-Vietnam War protests by newspapers, magazines, and television. The government put him under surveillance, delayed his green card request, and denied him US residency status. Despite facing harassment, public pressure rallied to his defense, and after many newspaper articles, the government granted him permanent residency.

Kim Kardashian is a more recent example of the power and influence of the burgeoning online social media. Her explicit sex tape with her then-boyfriend, Ray J., received massive coverage in both the legacy media and social media. The extensive media coverage made her so popular that the cable streaming *E* network gave her her own show, *Keeping Up with the Kardashians*. It ran for 20 seasons and is currently airing on Hulu. Kim also leveraged her fame into successful business ventures in cosmetics, fragrances, and clothing. She became the first online social influencer.

Kim Kardashian and John Lennon were both pioneers in their respective fields. Today, platforms like Facebook, YouTube, Instagram, and TikTok have transformed traditional media with immediate news coverage, two-way communication, and direct access to celebrities. [14, 16, 18, 22]

Users of these digital platforms focus primarily on the present, and their designers and owners make money when users use their sites. And the more outrageous their content, the more clicks they receive. [14, 16, 18, 22]

In this attention-driven economy, the interests and concerns of older adults will never be given the focus they deserve. The absence of older individuals on social media platforms reinforces the perception that we are expendable or even non-existent. [14, 16, 18]

FIGHTING THE PERVASIVE MISINFORMATION ON THE MEDIA

I recently watched Mariann Aalda's TEDx Talk, *Ageism Is A Bully: Stand Up To It* (2020). She said, "If you don't want to be invisible, shine." The suggestions below are ways to shine. [1, 3, 10, 11, 17]

- Learn about media literacy and the tools/skills that help you understand everything you see, hear, and read in the media. Take classes, read, and use YouTube tutorials. Pay close attention to the language, imagery, underlying theme/narrative, and who is relegated to minor parts. This information can help you challenge the misinformation about older adults. You can also take technology classes to familiarize yourself with social media and its uses. [1, 3, 10, 11, 17]

- Discuss ageism with your friends and colleagues of all ages. You will likely find that they are open to being informed about how people in certain age groups are depicted. Levy suggests these conversations will also help others feel more positively about the idea of aging. [1, 3, 10, 11, 17]

- Boycott shows that depict older adults in ageist ways. Spread the word through discussions with others, whether online or in person, and start a letter writing campaign. Write a letter to the particular network or streaming service informing them of your opinion of their content. Have others join in the letter campaign. [1, 3, 10, 11, 17]

- Utilize social media platforms to share your experiences and information about ageism. Publicize shows, podcasts, films that positively portray aging adults and call out those that don't. On these platforms, you can openly discuss how the media promotes ageist ideas about older adults. [1, 3, 10, 11, 17]

- Subscribe to AARP. Their print and online materials are informative and supportive. [1, 3, 10, 11, 17]

Completing any one of these activities will also help you recognize the ageist beliefs you have internalized. With this knowledge, you can redefine and better understand who you are. [1, 11, 17]

Before writing this book, I didn't pay much attention to ageist stereotyping of older adults, even though I had experienced it myself. Now, I recognize how ageism in the media leads to the stereotyping of older adults. I promise with this book and other similar efforts to make a change.

There are many older adults, from celebrities to everyday people, who have risen to prominence on social media platforms. I recommend one of my favorite singers, Dionne Warwick (@dionnewarwick) on the X platform. She uses the platform to share her opinion on current cultural topics and events. For example, during a show by a popular rap singer, she responded to a man who pushed aside a woman to steal the spotlight. She questioned the audience's etiquette and the event's lack of security.

The author Stephen King (@StephenKing) also has a presence on the X platform. He discusses literature, politics, and current events.

Baddie Winkle (@baddiewinkle) is a social media star in her 90s who uses her platform to challenge others' expectations about older adults and encourages older adults to live life to the fullest.

On Instagram, there are many older influencers who are making a name for themselves in spaces that are typically dominated by younger users, such as fashion and fitness. It demonstrates that there is a real desire to see influencers from all different age groups on this platform.

Margaret Chola (@legendary_glamma) and her granddaughter, Diana Kaumba, shares pictures of Margaret in stunning, modern, and expressive fashion. Chola challenges the ageist belief that older adults have no fashion sense and have given up on life.

Lyn Slater (@iconaccidental) also challenges ageism by advising her followers to embrace their age, find purpose, continue to be creative, and find different ways to express themselves.

Finally, Joan MacDonald (@trainwithjoan) is an older fitness specialist who inspires older adults to follow her fitness regimen, develop muscle, eat healthy, and remain independent.

I recently created an Instagram account and posted a picture of myself with my guitar. Within seconds, I received messages from people I hadn't spoken to in years.

We must make ourselves visible and assert our rights, just as many other marginalized communities have fought and protested for their rights. We must fight for our beliefs and demand the respect we deserve.[17]

In my fight, I openly defy ageist beliefs. I continue playing in a band and performing shows. I exercise six times a week and motivate younger people to do the same. I have written and published a memoir and continue writing today. I enjoy traveling the world and seeing new places, including my favorite city, Florence. I got married for the first time when I was 72.

Now in my seventies, I have accomplished a lot, but I still have more goals to pursue. I want to play jazz guitar, box for three rounds, discuss publishing and writing with older adults, and enjoy life with my wonderful wife.

Some days are honestly a challenge, but I rely on the skills I developed over the years. And once I'm out that door, I do it. You can have the same success when you remind yourself that *there is still more to do* and leave behind any doubts because of your age.

CHAPTER 5

THE ANTI-AGING SCAM

A TELEVISION COMMERCIAL: FOREVER YOUNG ANTI-AGING CREAM

Scene: A brightly lit studio in Los Angeles. The host, a young man with tanned skin, shining white teeth, and perfectly styled blond hair, stands in front of a table with bottles of Forever Young Anti-Aging Cream.

Host: Do you feel old with your loose grey hair? Do you have ugly wrinkles on that once-young face? Do you hate looking in the mirror in the morning? Well, I have an answer to your self-deprecation. It's a miracle: the incredible Forever Young Anti-Aging Cream. YES! You can look young again.

The camera cuts to 'before' and 'after' photos of the actress, a 65-year-old woman. In the 'before' photo, she has exaggerated wrinkles, dark circles around her eyes, and a deep frown. In the 'after' picture, the actress looks 20 again with no wrinkles, no dark circles under her eyes, and is now smiling brightly.

Voiceover: With our special unicorn-horn dust, you can be young again in just minutes! Say goodbye to ugly wrinkles, hideous dark circles, and under-eye bags. You can be ageless! You can fight the disease of aging.

Host: Folks, I have a surprise! If you order now, we will throw in a bonus jar of Peter Pan Forever face cream free. We want you to defeat the aging process.

Cut to the screen: Five older adults dressed in workout gear jump for joy.

Voiceover: Don't let being old get you down anymore. Become ageless with eternal beauty with Forever Young Anti-Aging Cream.

This parody of an anti-aging cream illustrates an example of marketing employed by the beauty industry. Other successful advertising techniques often appeal to consumers' fear of aging, incorporate scientific jargon to enhance credibility, exaggerate benefits, and feature celebrities to endorse product effectiveness. [6, 8, 20]

The corporate beauty industry exploits the public's belief that aging is a loss and a disease. The beauty industry claims that their products prevent this loss. You often hear or see words like 'reclaim', 'restore', 'reverse', 'eliminate', and 'turn back time'. The message is simple: not buying the product means neglecting yourself. [4, 6, 8, 20-21]

Their ads concentrate on the physical signs of aging: wrinkles, grey hair, liver spots, sagging skin, and losing teeth. In truth, these are perfectly normal and harmless parts of the aging process that don't inherently need to be 'fixed'. [4, 6, 8, 20-21]

The belief that growing old is bad is a social construct which emerges from everyday interactions, cultural traditions, laws, education, and social media. The influential media, including influencers, podcasts, Instagram, TikTok, and Facebook, promote the idea and make it widely known. Institutions such as the government, school systems, and, more importantly, social media reinforce the idea and reward behaviors that fit the newly accepted belief while punishing those that do not. [1, 10, 20,]

The idea becomes deeply ingrained in society's belief system and affects how we think, interact with each other, and shape our life's goals. In short, an unfamiliar concept evolves into a normalized way of seeing and understanding life's everyday occurrences – it's possible, even necessary, to stop the aging process. [1, 10, 20]

In the latest update for 2024, consumer agencies estimated the global beauty and personal care industry to be worth approximately $648.6 billion. In the United States, consumer agencies project consumers will spend about $104.10 billion in 2025. These figures support what the writer Ashton Applewhite writes about this industry: *'there is gold in the grey'*. [1, 8, 10, 20]

THE ORIGIN OF BEAUTY STANDARDS

THE ENGLISH APPROACH TO SKINCARE AND ANTI-AGING EFFECT ON THE AMERICAN COLONIES

Elizabeth I of England may have been one of the first people to go to extraordinary lengths to defeat aging, potentially as a way to maintain her power. Early in her reign (1558-1603), she realized that appearance, vitality, and youth symbolized power. Therefore, she adopted a rigorous skincare and anti-aging practice.

When you see portraits of Elizabeth I, you will recognize her flawless, porcelain-white complexion. Unfortunately, Elizabeth wasn't aware of the harm she was doing to her body and health.

What mattered the most was concealing the effects of life and aging on her face and body. [5, 14-15, 17, 20, 22]

Let's examine eight products she used to remain young and engaged.

- White lead (Venetian ceruse) was used to cover her smallpox scars on her face and neck. Sounds practical and helpful? No! The use of this substance caused severe skin damage, hair loss, and tooth decay as a result of lead poisoning. Interestingly, Parliament declared ceruse to be a poison several decades after her reign. [5, 14-15, 20, 22]

- Cinnabar/vermillion helped create her famous red lips and rosy blush. However, the mercury in cinnabar is highly poisonous and likely caused her irritability, memory loss, and depression she suffered in the later stages of her life.

- Kohl, a dark powder, was used to line her eyes. She placed the powder around her eyes to simulate awareness and strength. Unfortunately, kohl was made from dangerous chemicals at the time and her continued use affected her eyesight.

- Belladonna, also called deadly nightshade, was used to dilate her pupils to make them appear large. It contained a dangerous poison called atropine. Prolonged use could lead to blindness.

- Sulfur was also used in her beauty routine as a way to help to bleach out blemishes and freckles. Its overuse caused skin redness, burns, and prolonged dryness.

- Turpentine, now used as a paint thinner, was also used to lighten her skin and fade blemishes. However, it caused severe skin irritation, burns, inflammation, and, if inhaled, lung damage.

- Alum cleanser removed the layers of makeup Elizabeth used on her face. It peeled off layers of skin, leaving her face raw and irritated, introducing the highly poisonous mercury deep into her facial pores.

Elizabeth I became the first influencer because many of her contemporaries adopted her use of chemicals to defeat aging and the stress of daily life. Her make-up trends influenced the English upper-class subjects. They wanted their appearances to reflect the elegance and power their queen represented. Like their queen, they did not know the long-term effects of their beauty products. [15, 20, 22, 23]

The American colonies learned about English cosmetics from books and letters about Elizabeth and her court. They imported perfumes and cosmetics, which became popular through newspapers, gossip, and personal observation. The influence of social media has historical roots, and successful and influential people have always helped shape trends and connect with people on a personal level. [15, 19]

While America was involved in the Civil War, England was amid the Victorian Era. Both women and men were blind followers of the standards for beauty. Women had to have hourglass figures, long hair, and a youthful pallor. The women used skincare products, such as face powders and rouge, to make their facial skin pale, smooth, and delicate, free of suntan, blemishes, and freckles, with a rosy bloom in their cheeks. [3, 23]

They used the same cosmetics as the previously fashionable generation – powders, rouge, and fragrances which still contained harmful substances such as lead, mercury, and arsenic. Their frequent usage often produced memory loss, irritability, skin irritation, digestive issues, and fatigue. Despite these dangers, the desire to appear youthful and vibrant took precedence. [23]

The men followed suit, using powders, perfumes, beard oils, waxes, and pomades to soften and style their beards and mustache. They dyed their hair and beards to hide the grey, maintaining an image of bravery, strength, and loyalty to their beliefs. Again, similar to the women, their youthful appearance was more important than their health. [23]

SKINCARE IN THE TWENTIETH CENTURY AND BEYOND

At the end of the 19th Century, we had the invention of the Gibson Girl, a creation by the brilliant illustrator Charles Dana Gibson. This image broke loose from the restrictive Victorian Age. The Gibson Girl was confident, independent, and an athlete who played tennis and cycled. [13]

Gibson created her to promote the lifestyle of youth with loose fashion styles that permitted her to move freely with grace. The Gibson Girl's youthful style inspired older adults to seek fashion and cosmetics to appear more youthful. These mature women, like many before them, fell victim to popular trends or fads that were impossible to achieve. [13]

The men at the time continued to rely on the standards previously established – stylish suits, well-trimmed hair, and fragrances – and, of course, not looking their age. [10] They wore black or grey long-tapered trousers, white or striped shirts, waistcoats, cutaway tweed coats, and tall black or derby hats. Older men also used cologne, scented hair tonics, and after-shave lotion which left their skin spotless. [23]

The anti-aging industry dominated the mid-20th century, as Hollywood actors rose to prominence. For example, Rita Hayworth was an actress who took extreme measures to maintain her youthful appearance and conceal her Spanish heritage. The Hollywood studios forced her to undergo painful electrolysis treatments for two years to alter the shape of her face, give her a higher forehead, and appear more feminine. She dyed her natural black hair to her famous copper-red color. [9, 18-19, 21]

Tony Curtis, a heartthrob for many teenage girls in the 1950s, had multiple facelifts and eyelid surgery, wore wigs and hairpieces, and wore trendy clothing popular among young adults.

The most fascinating development during the mid-20th century was the increase in cosmetic surgery. After the influx of advertisements and influence of Hollywood, the middle class had the funds to afford nose jobs (rhinoplasty) and facelifts. They embraced the possibility of looking young and its benefits in their careers and social lives. [2, 9, 19]

The popularity and affordability of cosmetic surgery took off in the 1980s and 1990s with the rise of self-improvement and widespread ad campaigns featuring beauty treatments. Consumers sought liposuction, breast augmentation, and Botox. These same procedures remain popular today, partly due to presence of influencers on social media who, in presenting themselves as everyday people, promote the ease and accessibility of these procedures. [6, 9, 12]

MARKETING

Marketing is a crucial component of the beauty industry's success. In the late 20th century and early 21st century, television, print media, and radio relied on market-tested strategies. They include the following clever and sometimes misleading statements or phrases: 'dermatologist tested', 'hypoallergenic', 'clinically tested', 'doctor approved', 'cruelty-free', and a promise that 'it will work in seven days'. [6, 8,]

The emergence of social media now has broadened their advertisements. Beauty industry promotes its products on Instagram, TikTok, and Pinterest. Influencers and celebrities persuade their followers to purchase products by sharing personal stories about their experiences with those products. Companies, in an attempt to showcase their goodwill, also assure their prospective customers that their products contain natural ingredients, are free from animal testing, use eco-friendly and sustainable packaging, and promote wellness. [3, 8, 20]

The impact of beauty standards on teenagers is now more significant than in the past. With the popularity of social media, they can unwittingly compare their looks to retouched images of famous personalities. As a result, they feel pressured into buying and using these expensive products. [8] This advertising has targeted teenagers and will become a lifelong pursuit of maintaining a youthful appearance. Another unfortunate aspect of this focused marketing strategy for teenagers is that it is dishonest and unwarranted. They don't need these preventative products because they are still young and just starting their lives. [16] Through market research, they created an unrealistic image of attractiveness, enhanced with digital retouching. We fall victim to this manipulation through constant exposure and buy products to ease our insecurities about our looks. It's a game of pursuing an unattainable ideal. [6, 8, 12, 20]

Of course, it is impossible when nobody looks like themselves. Psychiatrists believe that this frustration over appearances is one of the primary reasons for the increase in depression and anxiety in today's teens and young adults. [7-8]

Recently, I watched a family member's process of posting to Instagram. First, she took at least 20 pictures of herself holding a concert ticket. After about ten minutes, she narrowed it down to six pictures and sent these to her best friend. They both discussed the pictures and selected the final two. The entire operation lasted at least an hour.

I spoke to her afterwards, and this is what I learned: it took her about 45 minutes to select the blouse she wore for the photoshoot. Then 15 minutes for her make-up, and another 15 minutes to create the backdrop for the session. Then a quick five minutes to take pictures. If my calculations are accurate, including the selection process and discussion with her best friend, that totals two hours and twenty minutes. Why?

For the same reasons skincare companies advertise. To impress and seek positive reactions through likes, comments, and followers. Several weeks later, she told me she was trying to compete with one of her classmates. Apparently, this classmate had over 500 followers in her school. She felt pressured to outdo her classmate but couldn't.

The drive to meet this fictional image of beauty is driving force behind the marketing campaigns of these profit-driven caretakers of beauty. As an older adult, seeing this profit-driven force is upsetting. It has inspired me to finish this book and encourage my peers to discuss its impact with their grandchildren.

DEALING WITH THE INFLUENCE OF BEAUTY INDUSTRY

As I discussed above, the continued pressure of youthful standards and the fear of aging have existed for centuries. I have given this much thought, and I offer this advice. [1, 7, 10]

Aging is part of life; embrace it with the energy you use while working. Stay active and get off that easy chair. Stay in touch with friends and loved ones. It's likely that they appreciate you for much more than your physical appearance. Keep your mind active by reading, doing puzzles, finding a new hobby, or learning a musical instrument. Find a purpose and pursue it. Volunteering is a perfect start. Local schools, libraries, and community centers are great places to start. Take care of your physical and mental health and focus your medical care with consistent, preventative visits to your primary caregiver. Exercise, meditate, walk, and explore. A clear mind provides energy and positive thinking.

How do I come to terms with my age? It's more than accepting my age. I established three clear goals for myself during these encore years, which I pursue actively.

I knew wanted to write. I have self-published a memoir in 2023, and now I am working on this book.

Next, I wanted to learn and play music in a band. So, I registered for music lessons at a local school and have performed with a band for five school-sponsored concerts.

Finally, I disliked being alone in my New York City apartment. In 2022, I married my beautiful wife and continue to appreciate her and our family every day.

These goals provide clarity and direction for me daily. I relied on the social, cognitive, and practical skills I developed over the years, through work and school and general life experience, in order to achieve them. The difference now that I am retired is that I'm doing these things for myself, not someone else. This belief has been driving force in my encore years.

CHAPTER 6

MINDFULNESS

*The present moment is filled with joy and happiness.
If you are attentive, you will see it.*

Thich Nhat Hanh

Manhattan's Upper East Side features restaurants on every block for miles, offering Vietnamese, Indian, Mexican, Greek, and Italian cuisine and boutique coffee shops – even two Dunkin' Donuts. As an Italian-American, my favorite pizza place is Don Bosco's Neapolitan Italian Food.

When I first enter, I spot a glass display of pizza. The scent of the pies' special blend of herbs brings me back to the iconic Totonno's Pizza in my boyhood neighborhood in Brooklyn.

Like Totonno's, Don Bosco's features tables with red-checkered tablecloths and mismatched chairs. Pictures of stars from New York's favorite sports teams adorn its brick walls, and another wall displays photos of the Neapolitan soccer team – SSC Napoli, the Azzurri (the Blues).

The speakers blast a mix of top twenty unrecognizable hits, and even K-pop. One day, I'm hoping to hear a Led Zeppelin tune.

As soon as the waitress spots me, she asks, "Richard, coffee with milk and one sugar?"

I respond, "Yes, Maria."

She returns within seconds with my cup of coffee and remarks, "I won't tell your wife you had coffee with pizza again." I thank her and study the display of pizzas.

My delicious choices are: Margherita (fresh mozzarella, tomato sauce, basil, and olive oil); quattro formaggio pizza (a blend of four cheeses like mozzarella, gorgonzola, ricotta, and parmesan); prosciutto and arugula (a thin crust topped with prosciutto slices, fresh arugula, and shaved parmesan); Sicilian style pizza (a thick, square slice with a fluffy crust, tomato sauce, mozzarella, and often anchovies or onions); and diavola (a spicy pie featuring spicy salami, mozzarella, and chili oil or red pepper flakes).

Seeing the white puff of melted mozzarella cheese, the thin crust, the dripping red tomato sauce, and the green mixture of basil leaves gives me no choice.

I order two slices of margherita. I feel its quiet heat through the white plate as I carry it with my coffee next to the closest empty table.

I add two envelopes of Domino sugar to my coffee and take my first bite of pizza. Soon, munching on my pizza slice and drinking coffee became robotic. My mind shifts to my wife's current workload as a home health aide. I picture her working countless hours with patients with Alzheimer's disease, or cancer, or heart disease. *She's been so busy with her patients. Gosh, I hope she learns to slow down. I worry about her. She's so tired.*

Then I hear Maria yell, "Mrs. Gamoro, your pie is ready." I snap out of these thoughts and in just a few seconds, my attention returns to the coffee and the delicious slice of pizza. I even recognized that Madonna's 'Material Girl' was playing on the restaurant's speaker system.

Question: what happened while I should have been enjoying my pizza slice?

Answer: despite the delicious flavors of my pizza, my thoughts kept drifting back to my wife's demanding schedule. As a result, for several moments, the pizza was almost non-existent. Luckily, the fragrant, garlicky aroma caught my attention, and I returned to my slice of Italian heaven.

MINDFULNESS

I woke up this morning and read the news. Deportations, the wars in Ukraine and Gaza, local crime, and other scary and confusing events filled the heavy air.

I also learned that a close friend had just finalized his divorce, and his daughter hated him now. And that my young neighbor, a new social worker, struggled with an outstanding student debt loan. Another friend was battling depression and recovering from knee surgery.

Does this sound familiar?

Life has its difficulties, with good and bad days. It's essential to handle the bad while celebrating the good. Mindfulness is an effective way to achieve both. [14-15, 17]

Mindfulness is being present. What does that mean? McLeod explains it means noticing what is happening in the present, not ruminating about the past, nor worrying about the future. [10] For instance, while sitting in a small, noisy park in Manhattan the other day, I saw a golden retriever chasing a ball thrown by his owner. I put down my buttered bagel and hot coffee, quickly wiped my mouth, and focused on the dog.

I remember seeing a straight muzzle, dark and intelligent eyes, a black nose, short floppy ears, a thick tail with an upward curve, and a light gold coat. It lasted about five minutes, and for those precious moments, the craziness of Manhattan disappeared. My bagel tasted better, and my coffee didn't feel as hot.

Earlier, when I was eating a slice of pizza and drinking coffee, a more mindful approach may have involved:

- Biting into a perfectly baked thin and crispy crust.

- Letting the mozzarella cheese melt on my tongue.

- Slowly swallowing the thick, slightly sweet, chunky red marinara sauce and carefully sprinkled flavorful basil and oregano leaves over the slice.

Scholars have divided mindfulness history into four phases. First, mindfulness originated over 2,500 years ago in ancient India's spiritual traditions. It borrowed part of its spiritual side from Hinduism. The concept of mindfulness, referred to as *sati* in Pali, became central to Buddhism when Siddhartha Gautama, known as the Buddha, emphasized it in his teachings. He taught his monks that mindfulness is a vital path to enlightenment. [1, 5, 9, 12]

Second, the monks studied and practiced Buddha's teachings in their monasteries. Soon, the monks started teaching interested people about Buddha's beliefs and practices, emphasizing meditation practices and mindfulness for those seeking to change their lifestyles.

In the 19th century, scientists and Buddhists aligned the scientific principles of the time – such as Darwinism, quantum mechanics, and the workings of the mind – with Buddha's foundations of mindfulness, which include the body, feelings, mind, and mental phenomena. People in the West referred to this work as Buddhist modernism.

Third, in the 1970s, Dr. Jon Kabat, a professor of medicine at the Massachusetts Medical School, established a program for stress reduction. The Mindfulness-Based Stress Reduction (MBSR) program has completed the link between science/ medicine and mindfulness.

Scientists then measured the stress reduction achieved by individuals practicing mindfulness or meditation. The public responded, and many began the practice, leading to a widespread acceptance of mindfulness as a stress reduction tool.

Dr. Herbert Benson provided further scientific support for mindfulness by studying Buddhist monks' ability to control their body temperature (*tummo*) and manage oxygen intake. [5]

Fourth, communities for older adults, healthcare, education, the military, and corporations have adopted mindfulness practices.

The Buddhist monks developed the practice of mindfulness. To achieve proficiency in their practice, the monks engaged in daily meditation, chanting, and walking meditation, maintaining awareness with each step. They engaged in mindful daily activities with full attention and gratitude, adhered to monastic rules and lifestyles, and, most importantly, practiced *vipassana.* [3, 9-10]

Vipassana, or insight meditation, is a conscious awareness of your breath, bodily sensations, thoughts, and emotions – being tuned-in to the present moment. This daily practice helped them develop their ability to concentrate for an extended time. [1, 15]

WHY MINDFULNESS TAKES TIME [2, 13, 17]

The brain is constantly under attack to provide answers. It's as if there is a thunderstorm inside our heads. For example, to answer a simple question 'what type of new vacuum cleaner should I buy?', the brain tends to draw on three resources to answer the question.

- The Past: it traces our previous experiences with buying a vacuum cleaner. These experiences may involve brand loyalty, choosing a newer model, or purchasing another well-known brand.

- The Present: we have to solve it right now – drawing on intuition and current feelings. Many factors can complicate a present decision. It could involve discussing the pros and cons of a current vacuum cleaner, the urgency to purchase one (such as preparing for a party or holiday season), or a sales promotion.

- The Future: Take time and do the research to anticipate the future. Go on Amazon and read the reviews. Another possibility could involve a person imagining themselves using the vacuum cleaner to tidy up their home before a party.

As discussed above, deciding, in this case, to buy a vacuum cleaner takes time because of the competing influence on our thinking from the past, present, or future.

Today, the constant flow of information increases the demand for immediacy. As a result, we often neglect to think in the present – using mindfulness to access our current needs. After all, our Amazon account is only one click away.

Finding the ability to be present or practice mindfulness can be challenging in this relentless bombardment of noise. How do we include mindfulness in something like purchasing a vacuum cleaner?

We can do so by using a balanced approach to purchasing this vacuum cleaner. We learn from the past, acknowledge current needs (mindfulness), and plan for the future.

MINDFULNESS STRATEGIES

Special Note: Before I list strategies to facilitate mindfulness practice, it's important to note that mindfulness is a personal journey. It's impossible to be mindful continuously throughout your day. I usually select meaningful events that provide a needed emotional lift. Your mindfulness practice will be unique to you, and that's perfectly okay. For example, my mindfulness practice involves having a coffee break after writing for three consecutive hours. [14]

As I take my first sip, I close my eyes and sniff the gentle aroma flowing through the air. As I swallow the coffee, I feel the warmth spreading through my body. It is smooth, sweet, and has a delicious, nutty flavor.

As I pick up the mug, the smooth ceramic skin of my beloved cup from Florence, Italy. The cup is white with Florence's red lily symbol embossed on one side. I am reminded of the beauty that surrounds that magical city. I take a breath, hold it, and release it. I open my eyes and slowly finish my coffee.

Mindfulness has numerous benefits for older adults. In a recent article, Wang et al. (2025) in *Pub Med* and the previous work of Jacob-Zinn (1979), it was found that mindfulness led to a decrease in depression, anxiety, and loneliness, along with an improvement in cognitive ability and spirituality in their respective studies with older adults. [6, 16, 18]

After a mindfulness session, you might notice improved clarity of thought, reduced stress levels, and increased concentration. These are just a few of the many benefits of mindfulness practice. Imagine the long-term effects of devoting some time daily to mindfulness sessions. The potential for improved mental health and reduced stress levels is worth a daily mindfulness practice. [13, 18]

MINDFULNESS PRACTICE TECHNIQUES [2-4,6, 9,10-11]

Attentive Breathing: You can efficiently perform this simple technique anywhere, anytime. I prefer sitting instead of lying down. Focus your attention on your breathing as you inhale and exhale. I try to hear the air moving in and out, inhaling and exhaling. When my mind wanders, as it often does, I gently refocus on my breathing. It's a straightforward practice that helped me navigate some trying times.

Another favorite technique is diaphragmatic breathing, which emphasizes using the diaphragm to promote relaxation. Another method, known as the 'breath of peace', involves inhaling through the nose, pausing briefly, and exhaling slowly.

Last is box breathing, which includes four equal steps: inhaling, holding the breath, exhaling, and holding again, each lasting about four seconds for a balanced rhythm. It is called box breathing because each step requires the same amount of time, like the equal sides of a square.

Digital Picture Worship: I use this technique when a thunderstorm vibrates inside of my head – when I am feeling nervous, stressed or scared.

First, I will open the Photos app on my iPhone. I select my favorite picture of my wife – she is standing outside in the late August afternoon in front of the entrance to the inspiring Uffizi Gallery in Florence, Italy.

Second, I focus on her smile and realize how happy she is.

Third, my focus turns to her captivating, deep brown eyes. I find the sparkle I love.

Fourth, I shift my attention to her hair. I appreciate its dark black color, its sleek, shiny texture, and it falls gently on her, brushing the top of her shoulders.

Last, I bring the digital picture close to me, about six inches away, and reflect on the happiness she radiates. You can select any image for this exercise. The aim is to help you shift your attention to small, positive details from a photo that you love. With continued practice, you can repeat the process with other images when needed.

The Word Stare: I developed this technique myself after encountering the term 'umami' (a Japanese word meaning savory or delicious) during my research for another writing project. After understanding its meaning, I wrote it down on a legal pad: I drew an oval shape around it. During the drawing, I looked at each letter; it was easy because of its unusual spelling – u/m/a/m/i/.

I studied the word and subvocalized its letter's name. Next, I listed five associative words: taste, recipes, delicious, cooking, and rich. Finally, I mixed up the letters and created unfamiliar words such as 'ma', 'mum', and 'mi'.

You can select fascinating words from books, newspapers, or films. The key is to play with letters.

Magic Eating – The Croissant: This technique works well mid-morning – when you have lost energy or patience. I often use a croissant, but you can use any food.

Place the food on a plain, white plate. Examine the food before you eat. For a croissant, I might see a brown crust, flaky layers, soft ridges, and feel a temptation to eat more than one.

Take a small piece, chew slowly, savor the flavors, close your eyes, and swallow – savor the buttery taste and enjoy. Repeat the process.

This exercise focuses on taste. It helps center and direct my attention after a concentrated morning writing session. It also helps me find a moment of peace, even while sitting in a Starbucks coffee hangout. [2-4, 6, 10-11]

Noticing the Small Things: Living in New York City, amid the craziness, has made this technique a necessity. It requires practice, but it works. I walk down a street in my Manhattan neighborhood full of traffic noise, construction work, music blaring from a car's open window, or people talking on their cell phones.

I find something that grabs my attention. It has to bring a smile to your face – a father holding hands with his daughter, a dog enjoying her walk with her owner, or an enthusiastic conversation between two friends. While walking, I visualize the image and let the joy radiate through my body. It is a tender moment that fills me with the realization that there is still hope in this world. After a few seconds, I quicken my pace and let the inner smile help me cope with the noise and crowds of the city. [2]

When I feel disoriented, I turn to mindfulness to refocus on what truly matters: my wife, my family, and the natural beauty around us – even in Manhattan. [2]

When you succeed, you increase your emotional resilience, reduce stress, and enhance your mental health – which leads to better brain functioning, memory, and decision-making. It might take time, but it is worth the effort. [6, 1]

For example, while revising this chapter today, I sensed a loss of energy and became distracted by the music slipping out of someone's earbuds. I stopped working and left the room to escape to the nearby park.

I found an empty bench, sat, and glanced at the cloudless, blue spring sky. After several seconds, I took a sip of coffee and looked at the sky again. I then began the box breathing technique referred to above – inhaling, holding the breath, exhaling, and inhaling again, each lasting about four seconds for a balanced rhythm. [10-11]

After about thirty minutes, I returned to my seat and resumed writing. My mind was clear, my energy restored, and the guy with the earbuds was gone.

As I explored the teachings of Buddha in this chapter, I felt it would be helpful to revisit one of his key principles. The following quote encapsulates this idea: "Your worst enemy cannot harm you as much as your own unguarded thoughts." [1] Incorporating mindfulness into your daily routine can help you manage your thoughts and return to the present. If you don't, you could lose out on an unexpected opportunity that brings you joy.

CHAPTER 7

CONTINUOUS LEARNING

Anyone who stops learning is old, whether twenty or eighty.
Anyone who keeps learning stays young.

Henry Ford

A few months into retirement, I visited my childhood home in Brooklyn's Gravesend neighborhood. This area, known for its two-story houses, beautiful gardens, and Italian community, is important in my personal growth. It has changed over the years, now welcoming many immigrants from China, Japan, and Eastern Europe.

Standing before my childhood home, I noticed someone had replaced my father's garden with a cold two-story house that evoked memories of my frozen winters.

Without realizing it, tears accumulated and flowed down my cheeks. A series of memories passed in front of my eyes. I could still recall sitting with my father in his garden on a Sunday, a spring afternoon. He told me, "Richard, don't listen to your fellow teachers. You do what you think is right. I know you. Your heart is always in the right place. Follow what you think is right. That's all."

I left my childhood home and passed by the church and school I attended. I spotted my old Boy Scouts' meeting place and I thought of my close friend Andrew, who passed away when we were both thirteen. Along with this sad remembrance, memories of nuns hitting us with yardsticks also found their way into my conscious mind.

On the way home to my apartment on the subway, I couldn't focus on reading my book. In my mind, I kept reliving my experiences and events from my childhood well into my early twenties. My anxiety about attending public high school without my grammar school friends, my first time learning to play guitar after seeing the Beatles on the Ed Sullivan Show, and noticing the tension between my mother and father throughout my childhood. After dinner that night, at my desk, I listed several of these events.

The next day, list in hand, I went to my local library and spoke to a librarian. I'd known Mary for several years so, over a cup of coffee, we discussed my retirement.

"What will you do with all this extra time now?" she asked.

I hesitated, looked out the window at Bryant Park, and responded, "Mary, I will read, play guitar, travel, and go to the gym."

She frowned. "Richard, that's not enough. You need more activities to keep your brain functioning well."

"I agree. That's why I came here today." I took out my list and showed it to her.

She studied it for a minute or two. "What is this?"

"It's a list of things that happened to me while I was growing up in Brooklyn." She nodded and went back to reading the list. As she did so, I asked, "What can I do with this list of childhood experiences?"

After a few more moments of reading and a brief pause, she suggested I write a memoir.

I bowed my head, then looked up, and asked, "What is a memoir?"

She explained, elaborated by showing me information from an online search, and recommended five books I should read.

I was afraid because I didn't see myself as a writer and felt too old for such an enormous project. Later, however, after two cannoli and a cup of coffee, I said a silent prayer and accepted the challenge.

Fortunately, I found some time to talk with my niece about how she begins her research. She mentioned YouTube as a good starting point, which surprised me. Previously, I had only considered YouTube as a tool for wasting time.

I took her advice and, after some procrastination, I was able to find some helpful videos on learning to write a memoir. That same night, I logged on to Amazon and ordered two books on writing memoirs.

Next, I needed to find a place to work but my apartment work area was smaller than a closet. The place I dreamed of had to have the right atmosphere for writing – long oak desks and chairs, desk lamps, ceilings full of murals, and a convenient coffee shop.

A colleague suggested the Rose Main Reading Room at the New York Public Library's Stephen A. Schwarzman Building, a short walk from Broadway and Times Square. After a quick subway ride, I visited the library and found exactly what I'd been looking for. I settled into what became my favorite space – the last oak table in the room's rear under one chandelier.

Every day, after a gym workout and a subway ride, I became a fixture in the historic reading room. I wrote and studied and, after several weeks, I gained a basic understanding of memoir writing.

Grammarly, a writing assistant software tool, became my immediate helper in developing ideas for my memoir. Trial and error (and restrained cursing) helped me tackle this uncompromising writing app.

After five months of reading, taking notes, and completing writing exercises and prompts, I began planning my memoir.

Finally, I started to write my memoir, which took two years to complete. Most of the writing took place at the library. Each day involved coffee, prayers, and a four-hour writing period with an hour for lunch.

During this time, I also read articles and watched videos about how to publish a book. The day I finished, I immediately began hiring an editor. However, I didn't know anyone in that field.

A YouTube presenter recommended Reedsy, a platform for authors to connect with publishing professionals. I browsed the directory of editors and began contacting them about my manuscript. I chose my current editor, who stood out because of her comments on my writing, particularly the tone, word choices, and themes. I had a strong intuition that we could collaborate well, and I was right.

Initially, after I learned about the Word editing and review process, her editorial comments and suggestions made me feel like an inadequate writer. After we completed revising two chapters, I realized it was her job to improve my work. It took us approximately six months to complete the manuscript.

I thought that would be the end of the process, but I still needed to format the manuscript, design a cover, and decide whether to hire an agent or self-publish using Amazon's Kindle Direct Publishing (KDP). Finding the right professionals to assist me with these steps took time. Again, I used Reedsy professionals for these services.

In October 2023, I published my memoir in paperback and Kindle formats. My family, former colleagues, and friends bought copies and shared positive feedback, particularly enjoying the chapters about how I met my wife and my high school days.

From the beginning, I knew the book might not receive literary accolades; however, I wanted it to be part of my legacy and inspire older adults, a reminder that we can accomplish great things at any age. It has given me a sense of purpose and the experience motivated me to write a second book.

CONTINUAL LEARNING

In his article about curiosity, Darius Foroux emphasizes that 'curiosity never retires'.[4] As we age, we often realize we partake in learning for others – in academia or in our careers, for example – but now, in our encore years, we can engage in lifelong learning for ourselves – we are in control of our education.

Remember the phrase, "If you don't use it, you will lose it." Our brains are like muscles. Your cognitive abilities will weaken if you don't regularly engage in new learning opportunities and continue learning. Like unused muscles, the brain will turn to flab.[5, 11]

Continual learning is the best solution for keeping your brain sharp and fit. [5,6] [8-9,13] It may sound intimidating, but it's more straightforward than it seems. An excellent way to begin is by trying something you've always wanted to do but couldn't because of work or family obligations. For example, you could try taking up photography, participating in writing clubs, practice yoga and meditation, join walking groups, take online courses at local institutions, or engage in educational traveling.

There are two distinct types of continual learning:[1-2, 15]

Formal: non-credit courses through local institutions of higher learning, community centers, and online courses.

Informal: You can explore resources such as libraries, community centers, online resources like TED Talks, podcasts, audiobooks, puzzles, book clubs, and museum and cultural center visits.

No matter if it's formal or informal, here are a few of the results of pursuing continuous learning [2, 11-13, 15-16, 17-18]

- Provides purpose and extended engagement

- Increases memory capabilities

- Improves emotional health

- Helps fight depression and isolation

- Improves adaptability

- Provides a sense of accomplishment

ONLINE CONTINUING LEARNING

YouTube: I explore its videos on many subjects. To access them, you can type the subject in the search bar and select the video that meets your educational needs. YouTube has a multitude of channels for continuous learning. Among the best are:

- Ted Talks are an excellent source of learning. I found these five sessions to be interesting and informative:

- *Embrace Age with a Longevity Mindset* by Helen Hirsh Spence

- *Aging is My Superpower* by Rita Moore

- *The Power of Active Agers* by Jeff Weiss

- *The Wabi-Sabi Path to Aging Happily* by Arielle Ford

- *Why We Should Embrace Aging as an Adventure* by Carl Honoré

- *GetSetUp* focuses on classes on using technology, health and wellness, cooking, art, and fostering social engagement.

- *The Art Sherpa* provides tutorials on creating artwork by painting with acrylics, including landscapes, animals, and fantasy scenes.

- *Senior Planet* from AARP offers tech classes, online safety, and fitness.

- *Bailey Sarian's Dark History* (a personal favorite) presents lesser-known and disturbing historical information using engaging conversation and humor.

The **AARP site** is an informative source which provides information on health, lifestyle, technology, and updates on Medicare and Social Security. [8-9]

Coursera is an online platform which allows you to audit (free) its courses and access lecture videos, readings, and discussions. Prestigious professors teach art, history, technology, and personal development classes. I found the following five courses both interesting and informative:

- *Responsible Medication Prescribing for Older Adults* offered by the Icahn School of Medicine at Mount Sinai.

- *A Public Health Approach to Hearing Loss and Aging* offered by Johns Hopkins University.

- *Knowledge and Skills for Dementia Care: The SSLD Approach* offered by the University of Toronto.

- *Healthy Aging and the Future of Cannabis Research* offered by the University of Colorado Boulder (Instructor Kent Hutchison)

- *Optimal Nutrition After 40* offered by a faculty member from the National Academy of Sports Medicine (NASM).

The **Khan Academy** is a free, nonprofit platform that offers interactive classes in math, science, history, economics, and personal finances for all ages — my sister, an art historian, is a consistent user of the platform. [3]

Here are five classes I am familiar with and enjoyed:

- The European Renaissance and Baroque Art focused on Michelangelo, da Vinci, and Caravaggio.

- Modern Contemporary Art focuses on 20th and 21st-century artists such as Picasso, Warhol, Yayoi Kusama, and Frida Kahlo.

- U.S. History covers topics such as the founding of America, westward expansion, the Civil War, industrialization, the World Wars, and more.

- World History covers topics from the earliest civilizations to the modern era. It examines relevant geographical issues, religion, trade, and politics.

- Writing: Informative instruction helping older adults write memoirs, articles, and letters to inform others.

Museum websites are excellent ways to tour museums from your home. Online virtual tours are conducted by experienced guides and can be accessed from each museum's website. [14] Here are the five that I found unbelievable:

- Vatican Museums, featuring Rafael's Rooms and the Sistine Chapel (Michelangelo).

- The Louvre in Paris, featuring *Mona Lisa* (Leonardo da Vinci), *Venus de Milo* (Alexandros of Antioch), *Winged Victory of Samothrace*, and *The Coronation of Napoleon* (Jacques-Louis David).

- Uffizi Gallery in Florence, Italy, featuring *The Birth of Venus* and *Primavera* (Sandro Botticelli), *The Annunciation* (Leonardo da Vinci), and *Medusa* (Caravaggio).

- The Rijksmuseum in Amsterdam, Netherlands featuring *The Nightwatch* (Rembrandt), *The Milkmaid* (Johannes Vermeer), and *Self-Portrait* (Vincent van Gogh).

- Smithsonian Museum of Natural History, which houses the world's largest natural history collection.

At the beginning of the chapter, I discussed publishing my first book, *Sometimes One Cannoli Is Not Enough: A Teacher's Life*. To accomplish this, I learned the craft of writing a memoir, working with an editor, developing a marketing campaign, and self-publishing.

My book describes my decades-long career in teaching and academia, along with my younger years and family history. It is my legacy and gratitude for being given the opportunity to teach thousands of kids.

When I saw the finished book, I smiled at the sky and whispered, "Thanks, Mom and Dad." I couldn't wait for my wife to come home to share it with her. Without her support, I never would have finished.

Many older adults are starting new paths after 60. Actress Judi Dench rose to global fame in her 60s. Diana Nyad swam from Cuba to Florida at 64. Frank McCourt wrote *Angela's Ashes* at 66 and won a Pulitzer Prize. Grandma Moses began painting at 78.

Whenever you feel uncomfortable or have the ageist belief, "I'm too old for this", think of the individuals mentioned above, including myself, who truly felt that attempting something at this stage of life was unattainable. We thought pursuing goals at this stage of life was impossible but we challenged this belief with courage and resilience. You have these qualities too – use them to pursue your forgotten passion or dream.

As you continue to grow intellectually, your strength will enable you to affect the lives of others positively. Please, use that easy chair for studying or writing, not just for sleeping.

CHAPTER 8

FINDING YOUR PASSION IN LIFE

Passion is energy. Feel the power that comes from focusing on what excites you.

Oprah Winfrey

On Sunday, February 9, 1964, my passion was born when I watched The Beatles performing on the *Ed Sullivan Show*. The audience, mostly girls, screamed excitedly, but my aunt couldn't help laughing. "How stupid," she'd said. "They look like girls. They won't last."

Despite my aunt's opinion, I connected with the songs, the long-haired musicians, the screaming girls, and the powerful guitars. It eliminated any doubts I had about pursuing music myself.

A week later, I bought my first guitar and began taking lessons. 60 years on and I still play rock guitar and take music lessons. Recently, I performed at three concerts held at my music school. I never thought I'd still be able to play 'Layla', 'While My Guitar Gently Weeps', and 'Still Crazy After All These Years,' yet there I was.

WHAT ARE PASSIONS

While I was fortunate to discover my passion as a teenager I've met many older adults still on the journey to find theirs.

Passion is the feeling that arises when you become so engrossed in an activity that you lose track of time and place. [2, 5, 8, 9, 12] For example, when practicing my guitar, the crazy chaos outside my New York City apartment window disappears. All I hear are the chords and notes that I am playing, and the time seems to fly by.

Discovering our passions can be challenging, as we often prioritize work, family responsibilities, and financial concerns throughout our lives. More importantly, the fear of straying from our familiar paths can keep us from exploring new opportunities. [1-4]

Dr. Dweck, a psychologist and professor at Stanford University, referred to this static, unchanging belief as a 'fixed mindset'. [3,16]

This fixed mindset carries over into our lives after work. If we allow it, life after work can become uneventful, self-destructive, and aimless. However, we cannot afford to be weighed down by negative, self-defeating thoughts. [15-16]

Dweck suggests that to grow as people, we must instead adopt a 'growth mindset'. This concept of growing cognitively is especially important for older adults. It takes effort, focus, and determination to explore and seize opportunities. [3-4, 6-7, 11]

For example, you learn that a local community group offers a yoga class twice weekly. You've always wanted to start yoga practice but never found the time.

This time, you decide to try a yoga class. If it goes well, you'll continue; if not, you can explore gardening, dancing, chess, traveling, or tutoring at a school.

You may also want to rekindle a passion but feel fearful because of a negative experience from the past – for example, perhaps someone laughed at your attempt at sketching when you were a young adult.

In this case, it's important to reframe that moment as a learning experience. Try engaging in that activity again in a low-pressure environment and focus on the present. Celebrate every minor success, build upon it, and surround yourself with a supportive group for emotional encouragement. [4-7]

No matter the activity, establish realistic goals based on your physical or cognitive abilities. If you are unsure about limitations, consult the person leading the activity. They can assess your current situation and help you establish your goals. More importantly, they will provide the help you require during the activity. [4-7]

THE IMPORTANCE OF PASSIONS

The Japanese embrace this idea of passion. They have a word for it: *ikigai*. It involves finding happiness in the activities you're involved in and sharing that joy with others. [3,6] This sharing is the real purpose of finding your passion. It is a selfless act that improves your emotional state and helps others with theirs.

Psychologists who study the aging process have identified the following reasons for having a passion as older adults: [4-5, 12-14, 18]

- It provides a purpose in daily life, motivates pursuing personal goals, and fills the void after our work life.

- Engaging in purposeful activities keeps the mind active and stimulated, helping to prevent emotional problems such as depression, anxiety, and loneliness.

- It fosters social connections and strengthens relationships. Sharing your passion with others helps them discover theirs.

- It offers opportunities for continuous learning, as you are self-motivated to deepen your interest by acquiring more knowledge about it.

- It improves the quality of our lives by giving us direction and fulfillment and reminding us that happiness and discovery continue as we age.

- It relieves the concern and worries of family members and friends about our quality of life as we grow older.

After I retired, I realized my identity had been built on my what my job was. Now, I could redefine myself.

I became focused on two things: playing the guitar and exercising. During my career, I had attempted to fit both activities into a ten-hour workday and handle other obligations on the weekend — such as grading papers, preparing for classes, and watching baseball and football.

Whenever I tried to find time for guitar playing, my thoughts returned to the pressures of teaching. I would often put down the guitar, escape to my leather recliner, and watch television or take a nap instead as a way to unwind from the stress.

Sadly, as a result, the guitar would stay in its case for weeks at a time.

As for my interest in exercise, it required little planning. I could work out because the gyms were conveniently located. However, there was no strategic approach during my working life, due to my other priorities; I exercised in a haphazard manner. As a result, my progress was slow and inconsistent.

After retirement, playing the guitar and exercising met my criteria for a fulfilling and purposeful life, and they became the passions I chose to follow.

I signed up for guitar lessons again, this time at a music school. My guitar no longer stayed in its case as I now practiced every night for at least sixty minutes. My versatility and musical ear improved significantly. I could play along with rock and jazz guitar backing tracks on YouTube. I studied music theory, learned to read music, and memorized the lyrics and chords from classic rock – especially the music of my hero, the great Eric Clapton.

It gave me purpose – I enjoyed carrying my guitar like a real musician. Learning music theory forced me to read, watch YouTube videos, and practice every day learning unfamiliar patterns and scales. I would watch a professional guitar player and note their hand and finger positioning and key signature during a music performance.

After several months, my instructor introduced me to several other younger guitarists and a drummer – an intergenerational connection. Within a few weeks, I started playing with a group. We have performed over five school-sponsored concerts. Our repertoire includes music from the Beatles to current selections.

The bandmates and I bonded over music and continue to rehearse once a week. My wife, sister, stepdaughters, nieces, and friends attend our performances. They can see the impact music has had on my life after work. My college-age niece Licata once said, "Uncle Richard, you rocked tonight."

My exercise program has also provided purpose, direction, and learning. Now, the gym is a normal part of my daily life. I work out at a local gym six times a week for an average of 60 minutes each time. [18]

With some guidance from an expert trainer and professional boxer guide, I am learning about the body, the proper mechanics of using weights and cardio equipment, and basic boxing techniques, including correct punching techniques and footwork.

Staff members greet me by name, saying, "Hey, Rich, how is it going?" Young people often tell me during my workouts, "Richard, your dedication inspires me." Hearing my name in the gym reinforces my commitment to fitness and health.

My trainer has taught me so much over the years and I have made considerable progress. Recently, my cardiologist informed me that my cardio-vascular system is now comparable to that of a 57-year-old male. Now, in my seventies, I am a proud gym rat.

My family, especially my wife, has noticed the physical changes in my body, including my improved gait and posture. I can keep up with her, whether climbing steep subway stairs or carrying packages from the local Target store.

Having a purpose, staying active, and continuing to rock has given me a successful third act.

IDENTIFYING PASSIONS AND OVERCOMING BARRIERS

In order to begin identifying your own passions, find a quiet place – for me, it was a quiet spot in Central Park in New York City – sit down, and jot down which people, activities, and places interest or excite you.

Think back to your childhood, adolescence, and educational life, and pay particular attention to events that stand out – maybe look at old photograph albums and note the activities where there is a sense of happiness and joy.

Reconnect with old friends and colleagues and talk about those times. Revisit past interests you neglected because of family and work pressures. Join book clubs and community center groups and appreciate the small things in life – sunny days, your grandchildren, or a cannoli. These activities will enhance your mood and make you more open to suggestions and new experiences. [1, 6, 10]

You may find a challenge in establishing an identity that was previously closely related to their work. One must overcome the idea that passions are innate and that a person cannot develop them with hard work and dedication. [12-13, 16, 19-20]

Change from a fixed mindset to a growth mindset regarding your abilities. Step out of your comfort zone and experiment;

remember that initial failures may occur. Be patient and use the resilience habit you have developed over the years. The fear of trying something new, especially after previous failures, is common but from my experience, we possess the mental capacity and emotional skills to overcome this challenge. [1, 6, 10]

Research others who have rediscovered their passions at a later age and flourished – remember Grandma Moses, Diana Nyad, Judi Dench, and Frank McCourt from the previous chapter. [21]

Get off your butt and explore: browse college catalogs, visit museums and libraries (especially the 700 section for arts and crafts), and stop in local community centers and look for events that interest you. Become a warrior against ageist beliefs that older adults are fragile, afraid of technology, unable to learn, or that risk-taking is only for the young. [17, 20]

Remember, like our work life, finding your passion is a process that relies on persistence, resilience, and flexibility – the same emotional abilities we have developed over our lives.

FINAL THOUGHTS

I finished this chapter after practicing 'The Last Time' by the Rolling Stones on my guitar. A renewed energy flowed through my tired body and mind.

Throughout my working life, my focus on education, career, and pursuing perfection had overshadowed my passion for music and playing the guitar. I came to terms with this realization after retirement.

Using techniques such as reflection and confronting my fears, I returned to playing guitar and taking lessons. In doing so, I've rediscovered the musician within me and plan to continue playing my red Fender guitar. My dream is to continue sharing this love of music with a younger generation and introduce them to the style and elegance of music from the 60s.

CHAPTER 9

TECHNOLOGY TO THE RESCUE?

Throughout Jennifer's career, she worked as a banker and retired when she was 70. At first, the transition was difficult. She had devoted her whole life to her work. Sure, she had colleagues she hung out with after work. But there were no close friends outside of work. She had spent most of her time at home, watching films on her Smart TV and using her iPhone to stream music. Of course, now she had more time than ever to do that. But she wanted something more.

One morning, she was overcome with a feeling of emptiness. *What the hell am I going to do today?*

She opened up YouTube on her laptop. She typed in 'European Traveling' in the search bar. She selected a video titled 'Spending Springtime in Spain,' showcasing various sights across Spain. She watched the video take her through Cordoba's beautiful courtyards filled with geraniums, roses, and petunias. Then the Museo del Prado in Madrid (which offered free admission for older adults at certain times) which housed masterpieces by Velazquez, Goya, and El Greco, the Museo Nacional Centro de Arte Reina Sofía, where visitors could see Picasso's *Guernica*, and the historic Alhambra palace and fortress in Granada. It also made mention of cooking classes to learn how to make tapas, as well as tips on train travel between Madrid, Seville, and Barcelona.

That evening, sitting at her desk, Jennifer planned a two-week tour of Spain. She used links from the YouTube videos that she'd watched to help organize her travel. She referred to TripAdvisor for reviews, ratings, and photos shared by other travelers about hotels, restaurants, special events, and deals.

With her granddaughter's help, she booked her return flight using Skyscanner. She learned basic Spanish using the free app Duolingo and downloaded WhatsApp to ensure free international texting.

Lastly, on the advice of her friend from the local community center, Jennifer used Google Maps to download offline maps of the areas of Spain she would be visiting.

During her trip, her iPhone was essential. She used Google Maps for directions, Apple Wallet for her boarding passes and payment cards, as well as accessing travel alerts, reminders, health insurance, and photos through other apps.

While exploring museums in Spain, she became mesmerized by Renaissance masterpieces: Fra Angelico's *The Annunciation*, El Greco's *The Resurrection*, and Hans Memling's *The Virgin and Child with Angels*. When she returned home, she opened up her laptop again. This time, she did a Google search for 'art classes for older adults in New York City'. Her focus was finding classes on the Renaissance.

A few weeks later, Jennifer enrolled in classes on the Italian and Spanish Renaissance at her local community center. She enjoyed the small class size, the conversations with other classmates over lunch, and the intellectual challenge of taking on something new.

After the classes finished, she decided to enroll in more courses, this time focusing on painting and sketching. She worked on portraits, still lifes, and Japanese anime.

It opened up an opportunity to connect with her grandchildren. They joined her on weekends to draw their favorite anime characters: Totoro, a forest spirit; Naruto Uzumaki, a boy who dreamed of becoming a hero; and Kiki, a young witch facing the challenges of growing up and dealing with everyday life.

Jennifer took time to find a purpose or a direction in her life and, as a result, became less isolated, more conversational, and more open to new advances in technology. It started with an impulse to travel. To find her way, she used two tools – one, overcoming resistance and the other, her available technology.

I believe that technology can enhance the lives of older adults. It has the potential to reduce barriers to accessing healthcare, improve social interactions, provide easier access to information, help keep our minds sharp, and enable us to age in place while remaining in our homes.

THE DIGITAL DIVIDE

We grew up without smartphones, Facebook, Instagram, or Zoom. I don't know if we were lucky in that way, but they are now changing how we live.

We must acknowledge the challenge and make the most of it. We refer to this challenge as the 'digital divide.' This divide represents the gap between older adults who own devices and are skilled in using them and those who do not have access or knowledge.[4, 7, 11-12, 16]

If older adults do not bridge the digital divide, they may face social isolation, limited healthcare access, and challenges with everyday tasks like paying bills and shopping. This can lead to reduced independence and missed opportunities for staying informed, entertained, or educated.

Besides the digital divide, older adults are also subject to the ageist belief that they cannot learn to use technology. Sadly, many of us accept this negative self-perception, which prevents us from attempting to learn.

Remember the phrase 'use it or lose it?' Brain stimulation involves continually engaging your brain in a challenging activity to maintain mental health and agility.[6]

Technology interconnects with brain health. Brain health is the brain's ability to resist damage and withstand age-related changes. The ability to fight off any damage to the brain during aging is called neuroplasticity.

Dr. Michael Merzenich explains neuroplasticity is the brain's natural ability to adapt, change, and grow new connections even as we age. [10]

He suggests that when we learn new skills, develop more memories, and engage in creative exercises, the brain creates or strengthens the connection between neurons – tiny cells in the brain that carry messengers from one neuron to another so we can think, move, remember, and feel. [10]

I see neurons as devices, not just connected wires. Imagine holding an extension cord in one hand and a vacuum cleaner power cord in the other; nothing works until you connect them. Once you do, the vacuum is ready to clean, and the more you use the extension cord, the easier and faster cleaning becomes.

No matter our age, the same principle applies when we practice a new skill, such as learning to paint. The more we practice, the stronger and faster the connections between our neurons become – just like when we connect the vacuum cord and the extension for the fourth time while vacuuming our carpet.

The more we engage our brains as we age, the stronger they can remain – similar to lifting weights; the more we exercise, the stronger our bodies become. Research shows that keeping our brains active can help prevent dementia. [12]

Benge, a cognitive theorist, states that the brain is a technological reserve that can help restore the energy we lose during our busy lives as we age. Like a muscle, the brain becomes stronger when we continue learning, enabling it to resist cognitive decline. [1, 3-5]

TECHNOLOGY-COGNITIVE BASED GAMES

Leung (2022) suggests in his article from *Psychology Journal* that it can be beneficial for older adults to play technology-cognitive based games. [10]

Older adults can access these games on their smartphones, tablets, or computers. These digital games maintain and develop critical skills, such as memory, attention, problem-solving, processing speed, and spatial awareness. [12, 14, 16, 18]

They involve puzzles, logic challenges, attention and focus exercises, language and word games, and activities that access how quickly the brain can receive and respond to information.

The activities keep older adults engaged and come with adaptive features that adjust the activity's difficulty based on the player's performance, eliminating any chance of frustration. [10, 12, 14, 16, 18]

He identifies these programs as helpful:

- **Lumosity:** This app provides fun games to help you practice skills like memory, attention, and problem-solving.

- **Brainer 1:** This app includes games that challenge memory, focus, and logic.

- **Virtual Reality:** These apps create lifelike 3D experiences – travel to famous landmarks, find hidden objects in daily situations, simulate social situations to develop social skills, and make settings from the past (diners, hometowns, old television shows) to help with memory and promote conversational dialogue.

- **Singfit** combines singing, lyric cueing, and musical programs to boost memory, speech, and emotional health.

STAYING CONNECTED

Technology can be a great way to connect with people, especially if they live further away, and to stay up to date with the world around you. Video calls, such as Zoom or Facetime enable 'real time' interactions with the people in our lives, allowing you to see the expressions on their face from wherever you are. WhatsApp permits you to send messages, media, and voice notes free of charge to other users in your contacts list. [4, 7, 14]

Voice assistants also provide alternative ways to socialize and connect. Amazon Alexa or Google Assistant are voice assistants that answer questions, set reminders, play music, and even tell jokes.

News services, including PBS News Hour, CNN Live, MSNBC, CBS News Streaming Network, BBC News, are often available online through websites, social media accounts, and even have their own apps, making it easier to stay up to date with local and international news.

Spotify and Sirius also provide news and podcasts that cover news, personal interest stories, and rebroadcast news shows from previous days.

HEALTH AND WELLNESS

Technology has affected health and wellness, especially for older adults. Telemedicine allows people to see a doctor or health care provider without leaving home. You can now have phone calls or video calls with a doctor using a smartphone, tablet, or computer. During this appointment, you can discuss your symptoms, ask questions, get a diagnosis, and receive necessary prescriptions – I prefer an email attachment. If I need a specialist, I use ZocDoc, an app that helps me locate doctors near my home or apartment. Before selecting a specialist, I ensure the caregiver offers a telemedicine option.

Medication reminders are made easier. Apps that alert us to take medicine include Medisafe, Mango Health, CareZone, MyTheraphy, and Pill Reminder. I use Medisafe because it sends messages to my iPhone and can mark my meds as 'taken'. [4, 7, 15]

Health emergency apps are essential in the modern age. These apps can notify family members, emergency services, and caregivers if there is an emergency condition suffered at home – falling, chest pain, shortness of breath, slurred speech, dizziness, or difficulty seeing or walking. Life360, Medical ID or Health App Medical ID, Noonlight, and iMedAlert are among the most popular options. [7, 14-15]

Health monitoring apps are useful tools that can track blood pressure, glucose, or oxygen levels. MyChart, Apple Health, Blood Pressure Companion, Glucose Buddy, and Care Clinic are the most popular options.

Similarly, diet and nutrition tracking are useful tools to monitor eating habits, track water intake, keep track of weight, and manage diseases like diabetes. MyFitness Pal, Yazio, Lose It, MyPlate, and Cronometer are among the most popular options.

Sleep improvement tools are also widely available to monitor rest patterns, breathing, and movements throughout the night, such as the popular app Sleep Cycle. Some provide guided meditations, soothing music, or even comforting bedtime stories. Calm, Headspace, and Pzizz are among the most-used options.

Finally, technology has revolutionized how we can receive mental health support. There are apps that can provide guided meditation, such as the aforementioned Calm and Headspace, therapy access, such as TalkLife which can connect users to discuss their mental health struggles, and tools to manage stress, anxiety, or depression, including Moodfit, Happify, and Woebot. Some local hospitals offer online webinars focusing on stress management, depression, and techniques to monitor mental health – NYU Langone is my preferred place for this service. [10]

PROTECTING YOURSELF FROM SCAMS

Unfortunately, along with the rise of technology comes scammers who prey on those they consider to not be technologically advanced. It's important to learn how to combat potential scammers and stay aware.

The most important strategy is to 'pause, reflect, and protect.' Identify scam triggers, such as unexpected contact, emotional appeals, and urgency. Take a moment to reflect on the situation and try to think logically. Then verify the source of the potential scam through other means than the initial point of contact. This strategy will prevent you from getting caught off guard. [17]

For example, your granddaughter calls you late at night, saying: "Granny, I lost my credit card. I can't pay for the Uber ride home. Please send me the money for the ride home. I'm cold, and I want to get home."

Unexpected: the late-night call.

Emotional: you care about your granddaughter and want to help her.

Urgent: it's late, she's cold, and she wants to get home.

Instead of rushing to send money, pause and reflect on the situation. Remind yourself: "My granddaughter never goes out on a school night and doesn't use credit cards." Next, protect yourself by hanging up and ending the conversation. Finally, verify by calling or messaging on her known number.

Another piece of advice is to never respond to an email from an unknown source or click on links within the email. Scammers create emails with authentic-appearing brand names, often using Amazon and various internet and mobile phone companies to trick you. It is important to note that in the US, Medicare and the IRS do not call or send emails to request information; they communicate using official letters sent through the mail.

Scammers may also text, email, or call, claiming one of your bank accounts has been compromised. This is another example where you can implement the 'pause, reflect, protect' strategy. Disregard the warning, despite its urgency about your bank account. Call your bank to check the account's status. You may also find it useful to frequently check your accounts to identify fraudulent charges. Contact your bank to freeze the account and the company involved, notifying them of the fraud.

Finally, if time permits, I will ask a family member (for example, my oldest daughter), a knowledgeable friend, or a former tech-savvy colleague to help assess the reliability of an email or text message. When I resolve an issue, I sometimes treat the person with coffee and dessert; if it's my daughter, hugs and kisses are always appreciated.

CONCLUSION

At the beginning of the chapter, I discussed Jenny and her use of technology. It helped her to travel, take online classes, manage finances, and lead a purposeful life.

Like Jenny, I have embraced technology in my personal life and in my writing. My favorite apps are Dashlane and You Need A Budget (YNAB). Dashlane helps me create, store, and protect my passwords, while Spotify lets me enjoy my favorite music by creating personalized playlists.

Meanwhile, technology has become an essential part of my writing routine. I use Grammarly for checking for grammar and style, Evernote for note-taking, Google Scholar for research, and Microsoft Word to write and review comments from my editor.

Using technology requires tapping into the intellectual and emotional skills developed throughout your life. If you take the first small step, you will witness firsthand how it can bring meaning to your life and ease daily stress. Imagine connecting with a close friend who has moved to the other side of the country or ordering a prescription online when the weather is too cold to go outside. The effort is worth the reward.

CHAPTER 10

EXERCISE

Exercise is so effective against the disease of aging that it has often been compared to medicine.

The first thing you notice when entering the gym is the loud, upbeat pop or hip-hop music bouncing off the walls. The younger crowd wears noise-cancelling headphones to escape the barrage. Meanwhile, we older folk make believe that we don't hear it in order to survive the onslaught.

Heavy lifters pump iron in the front area with free weights, while others use nearby benches for chest exercises and bicep curls.

To the right, serious gym-goers are at the squat racks. Two women squat over 150 pounds, showcasing their strength. On the opposite wall, six people use cardio machines like treadmills and ellipticals.

My trainer Jamie and I are situated in a quieter section, focusing on exercise machines, barbells, and dumbbells to work the legs, chest, and shoulders. Afterwards, I take a quick visit to the water fountain, and we move on to ten minutes of boxing. I'm lucky that Jamie is a professional boxer.

JAMIE: Come on, Rich, use the jab with your left hand.

RICHARD: I need to move my left foot to the side. Okay. Here it comes.

Richard makes an attempt at a jab.

JAMIE: Try it again. This time, move your left foot faster.

Richard looks up to the heavens and asks God for help.

RICHARD: Give me a second. Okay. Watch out.

The jab pounds Jamie's training glove with a loud snap.

JAMIE: That was it!

RICHARD: Here comes another, Jamie.

A second jab hits against Jamie's training glove.

JAMIE: You're getting it! Alright, let's stretch it out now.

Jamie has been working with me for over a year. We meet twice a week for an hour and I trained alone four more times a week. Yes, I was a gym rat. It was easy because I've been working out since I was a teenager.

As a sophomore in high school, I played baseball and football for the local community youth services. I developed my skills by playing with friends during the summers in our neighborhood park and street.

My father recognized my interest in sports and supported me by purchasing a set of weights, which included a barbell, dumbbells, and a workout bench. I feel fortunate and will never forget this.

I exercised in our basement four times a week and after a few months, I went from a husky teenager to a slimmer, muscular guy. The transformation improved my performance in sports and academics, as well as boosting my confidence in social interactions, allowing me to feel more comfortable talking to girls.

However, at my age, exercising is a way to maintain my health, mobility, and independence. Exercising has helped me develop a positive outlook and beliefs on ageing. For me, exercise is medicine and it continues to expand my interests and keep me healthy. [1-2]

AGING EFFECTS ON THE BODY

As we age, our muscles lose strength, making everyday tasks like climbing stairs, walking long distances, and lifting groceries more challenging. Our bones also become more fragile, increasing the risk of osteoporosis and fractures. [1, 14]

The heart undergoes changes as well. Blood vessels may lose some flexibility, potentially leading to high blood pressure, heart disease, and a slower heartbeat. Breathing can become more labored as lung capacity gradually declines, making us more susceptible to respiratory infections. [1, 14]

The nervous system also slows down, affecting our ability to process information quickly. Tasks that once took only minutes may require more time, and our coordination and balance may suffer, raising the risk of falls. [1, 14]

Hormonal changes occur during aging too. Decreased levels of estrogen and testosterone can affect metabolism, weaken bones, and affect sexual health. A weakened immune system makes it harder to fend off infections and may contribute to chronic conditions such as arthritis, heart disease, and even Alzheimer's disease.[1, 14]

The digestive system is not immune to these changes. Slower digestion can lead to common issues like constipation, reflux, and diverticulosis, while energy levels may decline.

Even our skin reflects the passage of time. It becomes thinner, drier, and less elastic. Wrinkles form, age spots appear, and collagen – the protein responsible for skin firmness – breaks down, causing sagging and dryness.

EFFECTS OF EXERCISING

- Increases life span

- Helps prevent cardiovascular disease

- Maintains and increases cognitive abilities

- Promotes healthy emotional health

- Increases immunity to diseases

- Maintains flexibility and balance

- Improves bone density

- Ease joint inflammation

- Supports the proper maintenance of body weight

- Increases opportunities for more social connections [8]

EFFECTS OF NOT EXERCISING

- Becoming fragile

- Loss of mobility and balance

- High blood pressure

- Emotional distress

- Cognitive decline

- Loss of bone density

- Stiff joints

- Loss of independence i.e. becoming unable to perform daily activities such as showering, carrying heavy packages, or getting out of a chair

- Loss of self-image

- Weight gain

- Shortened healthy lifespan [10]

MYTHS ABOUT EXERCISE FOR OLDER ADULTS

In her book *Breaking the Age Code*, psychologist Becca Levy explains that many older adults have internalized the ageist belief that ageing means decline and fragility. As a result, they believe that exercising is beyond their capabilities and an activity for the young. [2, 11-13]

Levy asserts we must change this mindset and keep moving. She writes that exercise and positive beliefs about aging are essential, allowing us to live longer with purpose. Here are ways to adopt a more positive attitude toward aging and exercise. [11-13]

Argument 1: 'It's too late, and I have never exercised before.'

Check with your primary care doctor for recommendations. They may help you find a convenient gym that supports older clients. The Silver Sneakers organization locates suitable exercise programs; some Medicare Advantage and Medigap plans endorse it.

Start small: mark gym sessions or exercise class dates on your calendar, track your progress, and set achievable goals. Avoid comparing yourself to others, especially younger gym members. You must be realistic and accept what you can achieve. Reward yourself when you see progress – visit a cafe or juice bar, buy something comfortable or fun, and share your success with your family or friends. [15]

Make it social. Join walking groups or talk to others between different exercises. I have developed friendships with older adults and younger members this way.

Get earbuds to play music while you exercise. Spotify and Sirius music apps have playlists for working out, and you can create your own lists.

Argument 2: *'I don't have the time.'* [2,4, 11-13,15, 18]

Reflection and commitment are the keys to solving this argument. Track your daily time by watching TV, browsing on your computer, or tablet. Cut it down and spend the time walking or going to the gym.

Experts recommend 150 minutes a week of aerobic activity (bicycling, swimming, brisk walking). That's 20 minutes a day, and you can break it down into two separate 10-minute sessions daily. Remember, an exercise program is flexible to meet your lifestyle.

Plan for breaks during travel, celebrations, or winter weather. Don't punish yourself for missing a workout and return when possible.

Argument 3: *'I'm too weak/sick/disabled.'*

A lack of activity causes frailty in older adults – it has the potential to cause more weakness or sickness. Remember, the longer we remain inactive, the greater the possibility of losing our independence. [11-13]

Please consult a doctor or physical therapist for suggestions and devise a plan with their guidance and support. Keep in correspondence with these professionals to assess your progress and make necessary changes. [18]

Hire a trainer to prepare a program that meets your needs. Remember, you are investing in your health to remain independent and live purposefully.

Consistent exercise, approved by healthcare professionals, will improve any physical condition, not weaken it. My trainer has developed a series of exercises that help with my balance and reduce neuropathy in my feet. He refers to this type of training as functional exercise. Its purpose is to make daily activities easier – carrying groceries, climbing stairs, or getting out of a chair. [14]

Integrate physical activity into your daily life. Take the stairs when possible or walk a few extra blocks instead of taking a train or bus.

When exercising at home, you can use everyday objects such as walls or chairs for support. You can find helpful videos on YouTube.

Argument 4: 'Exercise is for young people.'

We need exercise for the same reasons as young people. A consistent program results in stronger bones, toned muscles, increased mobility and balance, less stress/anxiety, and improved cardiovascular health. [1]

Avoid comparing your workout routine to younger individuals. Adjust your routine to suit your physical needs.

If you are worried about how younger individuals will react to your presence at the gym, consider going during the daytime when most people are at work.

Argument 5: 'It's too expensive.'

Consider it an investment in your health and lifestyle. Or better yet, ask yourself this – where would you rather spend your time:

sitting in a doctor's office or a modern, fully equipped gym full of movement and energy?

There may be local YMCAs or community centers with senior discounts. There are also city-sponsored wellness centers offering low-cost memberships

Check if your insurance covers gym memberships. Medicare Advantage Plans provide this coverage for gym memberships.

TYPES OF EXERCISE

Dr. Attia identifies three types of exercise for older adults: aerobic, strength-resistance, flexibility (such as stretching exercises):

Aerobic Exercises

Aerobic exercise strengthens the heart and lungs, making them healthier and more efficient. Examples include brisk walking, cycling, dancing (such as Zumba), and swimming. Light activities include moving around home/apartment, slow walking, cleaning, and standing up from a seated position. Remember to breathe out as you lift or push and breathe in as you relax. Avoid holding your breath. [1, 15]

Strength Training

Strength training helps to strengthen your muscles, which allows you to more easily lift grandchildren, carry groceries, and climb stairs. Examples include exercising with weights, such as bicep curls, and resistance training, such as chair or wall push-ups, or, my favorite, chair squats. [3]

Flexibility

Flexibility and stretching exercises are a must for older adults. They allow us to bend and turn quickly, improve our balance, and lessen muscle stiffness. Examples include seated spinal twists, neck, shoulder, hamstring, and hand and wrist stretches. Tai Chi, a form of flexibility exercise, boosts mobility-confidence, reduces fear of falling, and can help control arthritis. [4]

RESOURCES

I recommend the following online resources for information on exercise. [2, 11-12, 14]

1. The National Institute on Aging (NIA) developed Go4Life, an online program to help adults aged 50 and older maintain regular exercise and physical activity.

2. Silver Sneakers is a program that offers free access to gyms like Planet Fitness, YMCA, 24 Hour Fitness, and Crunch Fitness with a Member ID or digital card. Their app includes on-demand virtual classes, home exercise sessions, and workshops on topics like nutrition, mental wellness, and chronic pain management.

3. Senior Planet is an online learning platform offering virtual and in-person classes to help older adults with the basics of health and wellness, as well as other aspects of life such as technology, financial security, and social connectivity.

4. Vivo is a Zoom-based fitness program for older adults 55 and up. It offers small group instruction to build strength, improve mobility, enhance balance, and promote social connections. Instructors assess participants' abilities and tailor the program to their individual needs.

I have also found the following three books to be great resources:

1. *Growing Stronger: Strength Training for Older Adults* by Rebecca Seguin, PhD, and Steven P. Hooker, PhD. This book serves as a guide for older adults, emphasizing that it's never too late to start an exercise program. The guide focuses on activities that promote strength building, mobility improvement, better posture, and overall health. It incorporates the use of dumbbells, resistance bands, illustrations, progress tracking sheets, safety tips, and motivational tools as part of its exercise routines. [14]

2. *The Functional Training Bible for Aging Athletes: Improve Your Performance, Strength, Endurance, and Mobility* by Jordon Metzl, MD. This book is for older adults who have lifelong experience in sports. It focuses on functional training to maintain muscle mass, promote joint health, prevent falls through balance exercises, and improve endurance. Activities include running, cycling, and strength training with dumbbells and barbells. [7]

3. *Yoga for Healthy Aging: A Guide to Lifelong Well-Being,* by Baxter Bell, MD, and Nina Zolotow. This book is for

older adults who want to start or continue a yoga practice. It covers basic yoga postures and includes activities that increase mental clarity, stress reduction, meditation, and mindfulness – staying present for longer periods. The book features detailed illustrations, easy-to-follow tips, and suggestions for modifying activities/postures

I have personally experienced the benefits of exercise as an older adult. A few years back, I was diagnosed with CIDP, an autoimmune disease that affects the nerves. The disease causes muscle weakness in my legs, ankle stiffness, and difficulty with coordination and balance. The treatment involves monthly seven-hour intravenous of a special drug to prevent and help restore some of the flexibility I lost.

The doctors strongly recommended that I begin a regular exercise program. At this point in my life, I was lucky to be in good shape and had developed a regular exercise routine over the years. My only change after the doctor's recommendation was hiring a trainer, Jamie, to work with twice a week.

Jamie's training sessions blend challenging weightlifting and supportive conversation. He begins each exercise with a thorough explanation and demonstration.

As I watch and listen, I make mental notes to replicate the movements when it's my turn. When I attempt the movements, Jamie observes closely, counting my repetitions and stopping me when I reach a set number. If I make a mistake, he points it out and offers corrective feedback in an encouraging manner. I make the adjustment and complete the movement as explained.

His teaching method enables me to work out independently while following his routine. Other gym members often comment on my technique and dedication during these independent sessions.

I have made significant progress with Jamie's guidance and support. Before working with him, I approached the gym in a disorganized manner. I would only do the exercises I felt like doing, often neglecting those that were more challenging or time-consuming. Now, thanks to Jamie, I train with purpose, direction, efficiently, and without injury.

When my neurologist examines me, he observes my walking, balance, and improved reflexes; his smile and pat on my back are evidence of my success. Recently, my cardiologist informed me that my heart and its arteries are comparable to that of a 56-year-old man. I credit Jamie for this incredible news. Getting into a routine of exercising six times a week is challenging, but a spark of energy takes over once I arrive at the gym. Within seconds, the endorphins kick in. My body adapts as I'm working out, pushing through my exercise routine.

Another outcome will be the chance to meet others with the same goals. I have made several friends at the gym, and we often meet outside of the gym for interesting conversations over coffee at Starbucks.

If you are a stranger to a gym, I would advise starting with one in a convenient location. If it is too far, you will find excuses not to go. Speak to the manager or another staff member and be honest about your situation. Ask if they have a trial period so you can determine whether the gym meets your needs. Finding the right gym is like shopping for the sneakers — it needs to fit properly, look good, and motivate you to take long walks. If it is too small or too big, it will feel uncomfortable and you won't buy it. It's the same thing when finding the right gym for you. [15]

If the atmosphere, equipment, or staff at a gym don't feel suitable for you, then it's not the right environment for your exercise. It's important to find a gym that supports your fitness goals and offers a comfortable and welcoming environment that meets your expectations. [15]

It feels good when I walk home from the gym. I maintain good posture and stable balance, and my pumped biceps and stretched hamstrings leave me with the feeling that I did something good for myself.

To quote Dr. Attia again: "Exercise has the greatest power to determine how you will live the rest of your life." [1]

CHAPTER 11

NUTRITION

*There are forty thousand diet books on Amazon:
they can't all be right.*

It was 9:10 at my gym. I had just finished a 20-minute rowing machine session. It was challenging and exhausting, so I took a break and watched a boxing class.

Men and women were pounding bags, punching the teacher, and jumping rope. It was a picture of energy and controlled chaos. The average age of the class must have been in the mid-twenties. Their muscles and movements moved with precision.

As I watched, my inner dialogue went like this: "I wish I could do that. Look how hard she is hitting the bag. That guy looks mean. What a punch! I wish I could still do that."

As a 77-year-old, I understand and embrace my physical limits. My body, while maintaining a high fitness level for my age, has changed. Older adults need to understand the changes their bodies undergo as they age. It will help us meet the problems we encounter as we age, maintain our independence, and improve and prolong our lives.

COPING WITH BODILY CHANGES AS WE AGE

There are seven bodily changes our bodies undergo as we age and ways to cope with its effects: [11]

First, a decrease in metabolism is a primary change. Metabolism is the process our bodies use to convert food nutrients into energy. Dr. Attia and others have likened it to a furnace that allows your body to function. When we burn calories, we convert nutrients into energy. The energy produced helps us breathe, facilitates blood flow, and fuels physical energy. [1]

In our younger years, the system functions efficiently, entirely burning calories. As we age, our system slows down, causing the body to store excess calories in the blood ('bad' cholesterol) or the liver, which can lead to liver disease. When we have excess energy, we gain weight. As a result, we must increase protein and fiber in our diet, pay attention to the portion size of our meals, limit foods and drinks with added sugars, eat regularly, and not skip meals. [1]

Second, losing bone density causes *osteoporosis*. As we age, our bodies have difficulty forming new bones, and our bones become weaker. I have the beginning of osteoporosis. My treatment includes a special medication, zoledronic acid, which strengthens bones and reduces the risk of fractures. More importantly, I increased my intake of calcium and vitamin D. I continued with strength training and walking as part of my daily routine. [1]

Third, changes in our *digestive system* cause constipation, problems absorbing nutrients, and weakening our immune system. Potential causes include weakened muscles in the digestive tract that cannot effectively move food, difficulty breaking down foods, and allergic reactions to certain foods – lactose intolerance. Some effects are nausea, acid reflux, and constipation. [1]

I also have indigestion issues and have adopted several changes in my diet. My plan includes adding more fiber to my meals, staying hydrated, avoiding spicy and high-fat foods, eating small and frequent meals, checking if my medications affect my digestive tract, and exercising regularly. [1]

As we age, *muscle loss and decreased strength* become common issues. Potential causes are a sedentary lifestyle, a lack of sufficient protein and vitamin D in our diets, and changes in our nervous systems. [1]

I struggle with this change in my body. My trainer recommends adding more protein to my daily diet, including resistance training (such as weightlifting), balance, and flexibility exercises in our training regimen, and maintaining my active lifestyle by walking and cycling.[1]

Fifth, you may develop problems with *taste, smell, and diminished sense of thirst.* Decreased taste buds, medication, and sinus issues can cause loss of taste. Changes in nerves in our nasal cavity can cause loss of sense of smell. Lack of saliva, the body's system for detecting thirst, can cause a limited sense of thirst. [6]

My primary care doctor recommended these additions to my food to increase my sensitivity and appetite: herbs, spices, garlic, colorful vegetables, and staying hydrated even if I am not thirsty. [6]

Sixth, our *immune system* becomes less effective at protecting us from diseases as we age. One potential cause is that the thymus, an organ in our chest, stops producing the anti-disease cells necessary to fight viruses or illnesses. Our lifestyles contribute to other causes: inadequate nutrition, a sedentary lifestyle, elevated stress levels, and poor sleep habits. [1]

To offset the decrease in our immune system, we need to eat more vegetables, fruits, whole grains, and lean protein foods. We should also aim to get 7-8 hours of sleep nightly. [1]

Seventh and last, *dry mouth and difficulty swallowing* are present as we age. Potential causes include blood pressure medications, painkillers, dehydration, mouth breathing during sleep, and excessive coffee consumption. [1]

As older adults, we can solve this problem by eating softer foods (mashed potatoes, well-cooked veggies, and pureeing our foods), moistening dry food with gravy and sauces, using a soft toothbrush with fluoride toothpaste, and chewing sugar-free gum. [1]

OVERCOMING THE EFFECTS OF MEDICATION ON NUTRITION

- Keep a list of medications available to refer to when you need questions from a new health provider, issues with a pharmacy, or questions from your family. [4]

- Discuss in depth with your health provider the need and side effects of any new medications that are prescribed to you. Ensure that you understand fully how to deal with the side effects. [4]

- Make diet modifications or changes to offset the impact of certain medications. For example, if a medicine causes constipation, include more fiber in your diet. Or, if you need steroids, eat foods or take supplements rich in calcium and vitamin D. [4]

- Eat small, frequent, balanced diet meals.

- Exercise and stay hydrated.

EVERYTHING IN MODERATION

When I was younger, my mom caught me eating three cold pizza slices for breakfast. Instead of yelling, she took the slices from my dish and advised me: "Richard, I understand you like it. It's good for lunch and dinner. But too much of it is not good for your tummy. You must have moderation when eating food like pizza or fries or hot dogs. It's okay to eat it sometimes, but not too much. Capisce?"

Bless my mom. She was ahead of her time. She understood the concept of moderation in eating fast foods or processed foods. My mom never wanted me to deny myself the pleasure of eating something tasty but considered unhealthy.

Today, nutritionist Jillian Michaels recommends eating in moderation with the 80/20 eating rule. According to this rule, 80% of your diet should comprise vegetables, lean protein (chicken, turkey, fish), and whole grains (brown rice, whole wheat bread, almonds, walnuts, lentils). The 20%, the fun stuff, might be ice cream, French fries, potato chips, pastries, bacon, hot dogs.

Dr. Mark Hyman, an expert in a patient-centered approach to medicine, believes, "A healthy lifestyle isn't about strict dieting; it's about finding balance. Eating whole, nutrient-dense foods 80% of the time allows flexibility while maintaining health." [2]

The message is simple: don't deny yourself the guilty pleasure when you have earned it. For me, after a week of writing, exercising, completing chores, and eating veggies, fish, and chicken, Saturdays are eating for pleasure. These guilty pleasures include a corn muffin for breakfast, a pizza slice for lunch, and microwave popcorn with butter while watching Netflix. Of course, I am at the gym on Sundays. I can't help it; I'm a gym rat.

CREATIVE ALTERNATIVES FOR EATING HEALTHIER AND TASTIER FOODS

For *foods high in sodium*, I eat lean cuts of fresh meat, poultry, and plant-based foods. [8]

- For *sugary beverages*, I add water to fruit juices; I drink unsweetened herbal teas and sugar-free beverages (Gatorade Zero, La Croix Water, Coca-Cola Zero Sugar). [9]

- For *unhealthy carbohydrates*, I use wholegrain bread and pasta. Also, I have developed a taste for quinoa because it is high in protein and amino acids and helps boost my immune system and repair muscles. [2]

- For *trans and saturated fats*, I use olive or canola oil when baking and eat freshly prepared meals under the watchful eye of my wife. [2]

- For *foods with high sugar levels*, I have substituted fruits and limited amounts of dark chocolate. These high-sugar foods (cakes, cannoli, candy, and sodas) still tempt me, and sometimes I lose. However, as Dr. Attia suggests in his book *Outlive*, whenever I eat something like Dunkin' Donuts or French fries, I do it in moderation, and it's a conscious decision, not an impulse. I treat myself when I achieve a goal or need to remember that life is more than work. [2]

- Finally, for *fish with high mercury levels*, I go to a fresh fish market and buy salmon, sardines, and shrimp. We usually grill or bake the fish and rarely fry it.

READING FOOD LABELS

Below is an example of a typical food label. This fictional example was created to help you become familiar with food labels.

NUTRITION FACTS	
4 servings per container Serving size 1 cup (227g)	
Amount per serving Calories 250	
	% Daily Value

Total Fat 10g	12%
Saturated Fat 5.5 g	20%
Trans Fat 0g	
Cholesterol 30mg	12%
Sodium 825mg	39%
Total Carbohydrates 30g	14%
Total Sugar 7g	
Includes 0g Added Sugars	0%
Protein 18g	
Vitamin D 0mcg	0%
Calcium 300mg	20%
Iron 1.4mg	10%
Potassium 450 mg	10%

The % Daily Value (DV) tells you how much a nutrient in a serving of food contributes to a daily diet. 2000 calories a day is used for general nutrition advice.

5% or less is low, 20% or more is high

Ingredients: Chicken Broth (Water, Chicken Flavor), Cooked Chicken (White Meat Chicken, Water, Isolated Soy Protein), Carrots, Peas, Water, Celery, Onions, and Modified Corn Starch...

THE NINE PARTS OF A FOOD LABEL

1. SERVING SIZE

- *Definition:* the amount of food we eat in one regular meal. For example, if you eat three three-grain crackers, the information on the label is based on this amount. If you are still hungry and devour two or six servings, double all the numbers on the label. [2]

- *Why is it important?* It prevents overeating, ensures you get the correct amount of nutrients, helps you eat food in the right portions, and controls your intake of sugars and fats. [2]

2. CALORIES

- *Definition*: the energy provided by the food or drink our bodies require. For example, a piece of multigrain grain has 58 calories per slice.

- *Why is it important?* Knowing the calories of food and drink helps us maintain our weight and not overeat. [7]

3. PERCENT OF DAILY VALUE

- *Definition*: a number that tells how rich in nutrients the food contains. Nutritionists calculate it based on our daily intake of 2,000 calories a day. I follow the 5-20 rule. If a food valued at 20 percent or higher, it is good for me. If it is five or lower, I avoid it.

- *Why is it important?* It helps me control my intake of harmful nutrients for my health. If I'm searching for a breakfast cereal with a high fiber content, I will select the one with the highest DV value. [3]

4. TOTAL FAT

- *Definition*: are nutrients with two distinct groups: good (mono-saturated and polyunsaturated) and bad (saturated and trans fats). For example, olive oil, avocados, salmon, and walnuts contain good fats. In contrast, butter, beef, pork, cookies, and chips contain bad fats. [5]

- *Why is it important?* Good fats help by providing energy, promoting cell growth, protecting our organs, and helping absorb vitamins. Bad fats can increase the risk of heart disease and cause strokes. [5]

5. CHOLESTEROL

- *Definition*: fatty substance in the blood that could block blood flow in our arteries. For example, there are two types of cholesterol: 'good' (HDL/High-Density Lipoprotein) found in fish, nuts, and olive oil, and 'bad' (LDL/Low-Density Lipoprotein) found in red meats, bacon, butter, and cheese.[10]

- *Why is it important?* Both types of cholesterol serve a purpose but high levels of LDL can cause heart disease and may produce strokes. [10]

6. SODIUM

- *Definition*: more commonly known as salt – high sodium foods include bacon, ham, canned soups, potato chips, and parmesan cheese. [5]

- *Why is it important?* Knowing sodium levels in foods can prevent high blood pressure, heart disease, kidney damage, and loss of bone density. Nutritional experts suggest older adults consume 1,500 mg of sodium daily, equivalent to approximately two-thirds of a teaspoon of salt. [5]

7. CARBOHYDRATES

- *Definition:* nutrients found in food and drinks. They are an essential source of energy. There are two examples: simple, found in sugar and fruit, and complex, found in whole grains, vegetables, and legumes. [2]

- *Why is it important?* Complex carbs provide energy, contain high levels of fiber, lower bad cholesterol, and lessen the risk of cardiovascular disease. Simple carbs produce rapidly high levels of sugar in the blood, risk type 2 diabetes, cause cardiovascular disease, and lead to weight gain. [2]

8. PROTEIN

- *Definition:* a nutrient that supports the building, repairing, and maintaining our body tissues. Examples: found in meat, fish, yogurt, eggs, beans, and nuts.

- *Why is it important?* It helps preserve our muscles, fortifies our immune system, and makes recovering from illnesses or injuries easier. [2]

9. MICRONUTRIENTS

- *Definition*: these are essential vitamins and minerals that help carbs, proteins, and fats provide our bodies with energy – examples: fruits, vegetables, grains, dairy products, or supplements. [3]

- *Why are they important?* They support the immune system, help fight cardiovascular disease, and facilitate the body's ability to produce energy. [3]

IMPORTANT TO NOTE – HIDDEN SUGARS

Dr. Attia defines 'hidden sugars' as ingredients added to food to enhance taste or shelf life that are not always obvious from the food label. [2,18]

Manufacturers often use unfamiliar names to disguise hidden sugars. For instance, they may label high-fructose corn syrup as dextrose in processed meats and use brown rice syrup in granola bars. Agave syrup or nectar can also be found in granola, protein bars, smoothies, flavored yogurts, energy drinks, and honey mustard. [2,18]

Nutritionists often refer to foods and drinks containing hidden sugars as empty calories. Flavored yogurts contain 15-20 grams of sugar per serving (even for low-fat brands). Breakfast cereals include added cane sugar or molasses (check granola and whole-grain cereals). Ketchup and barbecue sauce have 3-5 grams of sugar in one tablespoon. [2, 18]

An example to remember is that a can of Coke has twice the sugar of milk but provides calcium, protein, and vitamin D.

TIPS FOR REDUCING HIDDEN SUGARS: [2, 18]

- Choose unprocessed foods.

- Select whole foods with simple ingredient lists.

- Follow the great-grandmother's rule: "If food has a long label, it might not be the best choice."

- Read nutrition labels and select items lower in fat, added sugars, and sodium.

- Discuss your diet with your healthcare provider and consult a nutritionist.

- Choose snacks and beverages with fiber, protein, vitamins, and minerals.

EXAMPLES OF SNACKS WITHOUT HIDDEN SUGARS ARE: [2,18]

- Protein shakes

- Protein-rich snack bars

- Trail mix with nuts, seeds, and dried fruit.

- Cottage cheese without flavoring

CONCLUDING REMARKS

My parents hosted many holiday dinners in their huge basement dining room. The menu featured a variety of Italian delicacies, including meatballs, lasagna, ravioli, roast chicken, veal and eggplant parmesan, plenty of wine, and luscious pastries. The dinner went on for hours.

No-one counted calories or the amount of sodium in the food or worried about their cholesterol. The food nourished our bodies and brought us joy and inspiration. It created a warm space for sharing conversations, culture, and love, reminding us of our deep-seated love for each other.

The same experience recently occurred with a friend. His 25-year-old son had recently been fired by a local tech company. As a result, his son went into a depressive state and required medical attention. The day after his son received a medical diagnosis of emotional issues, I had lunch with my unfortunate friend.

We, both health nerds, went to a local Greek diner and ordered cheeseburgers, fries, and Coke colas. While we ate, we talked about our days teaching in the 70s. Our cheerful laughter and enthusiastic fist bumps relieved the tension my friend had been feeling.

I sensed his relief and delicately started our discussion of his son's recent setbacks. Over coffee and baklavas, we arrived at a solution. We agreed that a former colleague, who is an expert career counselor, would meet with his son.

Several weeks later, the meeting occurred, and the counselor contacted various tech companies, one of which offered a job to my friend's son. He was also now seeing a therapist for emotional support during this transition.

There are times, even as older adults, when we need an escape to help us refocus our thinking and relieve stress. Dr. Attia emphasizes we should not impulsively deviate from our daily restrictive diets because it can lead to overeating and gaining unwanted weight. Instead, like my holiday meals or luncheon meeting, they must have a purpose and intentionally enhance our quality of life. [2]

If we can determine when and how we should alter our eating habits to fulfill our needs, it helps maintain our independence and control of our lives. I think of preserving our autonomy and establishing our priorities is the key to living purposeful and impactful encore years. [2]

CHAPTER 12

AGING IN PLACE VERSUS RETIREMENT COMMUNITIES

It is not how old you are, but how you are.

Jules Renard

TWO DIFFERENT PATHS

Consider the contrasting lives of Pamela and Jorge, two lifelong business partners in their early seventies.

A dedicated mother, Pamela has spent her life in the family home, nurturing her two children with her late husband. Her home is beautifully decorated with photographs and mementos from the family's many adventures. Now, having made the choice to age in place, Pamela spends her mornings gardening and her afternoons reading. After dinner, she watches TV before going to bed at nine every night. Recently, however, she has been grappling with a sense of isolation, finding it increasingly difficult to maintain her home and complete her daily tasks.

In contrast, Jorge felt isolated and alone in his large home after his wife's passing. He moved to a retirement community. He wanted to try something new that would help him regain some of the joy he had with his wife.

After a few weeks of adjustment, Jorge enjoyed his new routine daily weightlifting, yoga, communal meals, and the comfort of round-the-clock medical care. His children noticed his positive transformation, and he has rediscovered his passion for sports and reading. This transformation gave him a renewed sense of purpose and a brighter outlook on life.

Several months later, after emailing each other, Pamela and Jorge met at a local coffee shop.

Pamela drank her latte and noticed that Jorge looked relaxed and happy. "Jorge, how is it going at the retirement community?" she asked.

"I love it," Jorge beamed. "I have become really interested in practicing yoga. We have an instructor who meets us three times a week before our delicious breakfast."

"How is the food for the rest of the day?"

"Lunch is great! We usually have a soup and sandwich combo. And for dessert, fresh fruit or sugar-free pudding. For dinner, there is a meat or seafood option, followed by fruit salad or, my favorite, angel food cake."

"Wow! You are eating like a champ, Jorge."

"The best thing, Pam, is that I have access to 24-hour medical care. So I don't need to worry if, God forbid, I have a fall or any kind of emergency."

"You made a good choice," Pamela said, impressed.

"What about you, Pam? How is it going at home?"

Pamela smiled. "I love the fact that I still live at home. It's great to have my comfortable couch to watch the news and Netflix. I enjoy sleeping in my own bed, which I shared with my late husband. And in the mornings, when the weather is okay, I still love to garden."

Jorge detected some hesitation in her tone. "Pam, are you still happy living in your home?" he asked. "I'm just wondering."

Pamela paused before answering. "Not really," she admitted. "It gets lonely sometimes. My children both live far away. And I never see my grandchildren. I refuse to see them using Zoom. It seems strange to me. I can't hug or kiss them."

Jorge nodded understandingly. "I felt the same way when I first moved to my retirement community. It was hard but it just takes some time to adjust. I'm sure things will improve."

Pamela smiled at her friend. "I hope so."

Pamela and Jorge's stories underscore the weighty decisions many older adults face today. We must choose whether to age in place or transition to a retirement community. This decision will profoundly affect our quality of life, social interactions, and emotional well-being.

AGING IN PLACE

Many older adults choose to stay in their homes as they age, known as 'aging in place', because it provides them with a sense of comfort and familiarity filled with meaningful memories. It helps reinforce your identity. Older adults can still appreciate the familiar scent of their homes, favorite books on a shelf, and framed photos of their family. This familiarity can bring a sense of security and peace, contributing to their emotional well-being. They also value the independence and autonomy that aging in place affords them, which can boost their self-esteem and sense of control. In this way, it helps older adults maintain their independence and self-reliance in daily routines and outings and permits them to make their own decisions. [2-3, 1, 9, 13, 24 -25]

Feelings of isolation and loneliness are likely to arise while aging in place, as friends and family may move or pass away. Additional support services such as home attendants, nurses, or caregivers may be required in certain cases. Another solution is for older adults to preserve social connections in local communities such as friends within their neighborhoods, places of worship, or community centers as they age in place. [14, 18]

In some cases, aging in place could be cost-effective; however, unforeseen costs may arise, causing additional spending. For example, if mobility becomes an issue, people might require costly home modifications for better accessibility and safety such as ramps, chair lifts, walk-in bathtubs. Older adults may also need to invest in assistive technology to aid in daily activities, such as medical alert wristbands, cameras, smart door locks, and motion-activated lighting. The overall cost of these technologies can often be equivalent to living in an assisted-care community. [2, 4, 6, 9]

Another difficulty is accessing external medical care where older adults may rely on using public transportation, arranging car services, or rely on local agencies to provide home visits, which may not be a guarantee. Family members who live locally may be able to provide additional support but this can cause emotional and physical strain for them as they balance their daily lives (such as work or social lives) with family obligations. [2, 15-16]

Finally, declining cognitive function in older adults may lead to some serious issues for those aging in place and living alone. They might miss taking their necessary medications, neglect to turn off appliances like the stove, or, even worse, not notice the smell of a gas leak. [8, 16]

RETIREMENT COMMUNITIES

There are six types of retirement communities which exist as an alternative to aging in place for those who choose the option:

1. *Independent living:* These apartment units are typically more suitable for active, mobile older adults. Living here feels like staying at a resort for an extended period. Older adults can live in private apartments or cottages and must hire their own home health aide and others to assist with daily care if needed. They also have out-of-pocket costs for rent, housekeeping, maintenance, meal plans, and lawn care. Medicare or private insurance can cover their medical expenses. [8-9, 11]

2. *Assisted living* offers older adults private or semi-private apartments without the intensive care typically found in nursing homes. Residents take part in activities, such

as fitness programs, organized trips, and shared meals. Facilities include emergency call systems and staff available for assistance. People cover costs using out-of-pocket payments, insurance, and savings. [8-9, 11]

3. *Memory care facilities* are environments with specialized care for individuals who have Alzheimer's disease or other forms of dementia. They can be standalone or part of an existing larger facility. Living arrangements can include private rooms, studio apartments, or a shared room. They provide 24/7 supportive services, including preventive and urgent care, diagnostic services, physical therapy, and rehabilitation. Their primary focus is to create a place where their patients can experience dignity, comfort, and a sense of belonging. [8-9, 11]

4. *Private home care* is more aligned with aging in place. Caregivers help their patients maintain their independence. They provide these services, including assistance in activities of daily living (known as ADLs) such as eating, bathing, dressing, toileting and grooming. They also perform nursing duties such as helping to manage prescription medications, providing companionship, and lessening any feelings of isolation. The home care relies on personalized care plans designed to give the patient more choice and freedom as they age in place. [8-9, 11]

5. *Skilled nursing facilities,* also known as nursing homes, are places where individuals live and carry out their daily

activities. They typically share a room with another resident. There is 24/7 care and monitoring with a focus on medical care. The continued round-the-clock support enables individuals to focus on living a full life. [8-9, 11]

6. ***Continuing Care Retirement Communities (CCRCs):*** These communities enable residents to transition between different levels of care as needed. All services are available in one location, so patients do not have to travel. [8-9, 11]

COST COMPARISONS

Aging in place:

- *Home Modifications:* $1,000 to $10,000 + to ensure safety, accessibility, and comfort as the physical and cognitive needs change. These include grab bars for showers, ramps or residential elevators for assistance with stairs, widened kitchen aisles, medical alert wristbands, and motion-activated lighting. [4, 8, 26]

- *Continuous in-home care* costs range from $600 to $1,000 per month for part-time assistance and from $4,000 to $10,000 per month for full-time care. The services provided include help with ADLs such as eating, bathing, dressing, toileting, and grooming, along with support for shopping, medical and financial management, nursing care, and home repairs. [4, 8, 26]

- *Living expenses* encompass groceries, electricity, rent, mortgages, and payments for part-time care ($600-$1,000 per month), full-time care ($4,000 to $10,000 per month), and technology. [4, 8, 26]

Retirement communities:

- *Entrance Fees:* $100,000 to $1 million-plus. These one-time payments reserve a spot in the community and cover the cost of housing, services, and possible health care. The entrance fee can range from $100,000 to over a million. These entrance fees are refundable and specified in the residents' contract. [3, 11]

- *Monthly fees:* $2,000 to $10,000+, depending on the level of care provided and the specific type of community the older adult lives in. These fees include housing, housekeeping, personal care, organized activities, transportation, and help with medications. Different communities provide various services depending on the needs of their patients. [3, 11]

FACTORS TO CONSIDER WHEN MAKING A DECISION

The decision about aging in place or living in a community is more than about safety or cost; it's about living a life that combines dignity, happiness, trust, purpose, comfort and trust. There are many important elements to consider. [8, 20-21]

The health status of older adults, including whether they need continuous or intermittent care, is an important consideration. If an older adult is healthy, mobile, and mentally sharp, then aging in place may be the best choice. However, a community setting could be more appropriate if they require ongoing medical care, as many retirement communities provide 24-hour comprehensive care and supervision to meet their needs. [8, 20-21]

Safety and security are essential for aging with care and purpose. Aging in place sometimes requires costly modifications that do not provide immediate care and safety in case of unforeseen events like falls or strokes. In contrast, older adults in community facilities enjoy round-the-clock safety and security. [8, 20-21]

The connection and relationships with family, friends, and former colleagues are maintained. Aging in place helps maintain this closeness and connection to family, community, and former colleagues. However, the stress on a family member caring for someone aging in place can present challenges like caregiver burnout, financial strain, and physical and emotional exhaustion if the older adult requires more support because of an illness or a mobility issue occurs. Likewise, living in a retirement community can affect the older adult and family members, though in different ways. The older adult might suffer from the effects of a perceived abandonment and miss their former life at home with its memories and communal connections. The family and friends in turn will miss the established familial connections, a sense of loss, and perhaps feelings of guilt for their contribution to the decision. [8, 20-21]

Community engagement and volunteering opportunities are available for older adults who seek them out if they decide to age in place. Living in a retirement community also provides these opportunities. The purpose of the communities is to help prevent feelings of isolation and lack of engagement. They offer daily activities, group meals, and occasional trips tailored to the interests and needs of the residents. [8, 20-21]

Discussions on the decision to age in place or move to a retirement community, especially with older adults, must be honest and open. It's important to include the opinions of the health care providers involved in the treatment of the older adults, such as doctors, psychiatrists, therapists, and nurses. Trial visits to the retirement communities are an opportunity to learn more if this option is being considered. It's essential to consider older adults' lifestyle preferences. Generally speaking, introverted individuals may prefer aging in place, while extroverts often thrive in communal settings like a retirement community. [2, 8, 10, 12-13, 15, 26]

Aging in place allows individuals to remain at home and age with support and care. Retirement communities require people to leave their homes and live in structured environments with comprehensive support and care. While extended family members may become involved with this decision, it is most important that the older adult involved should make the final decision regarding their choice. It's their life, and they've earned this right. [2, 8, 15, 21]

Families should carefully plan the time when making this decision as it will significantly affect the quality of life for an older adult. The older adults must prepare themselves while their families will continue to love and support them. [2, 8, 15, 21]

In my research, the underlying theme is that aging is not a retreat from life but a different way to engage with life. Whether you choose to age in place or a community, the most critical factor in your decision should be that you feel supported and inspired to live a life with purpose and meaning. It's not about the location; it's about the ability to live fully and give back to everyone who has touched your life.

CHAPTER 13

THE POWER OF ART AND MUSIC

Last spring, on a Thursday, I felt completely detached. I was angry and worried about the tension between my wife and sister, which I had sensed during family gatherings.

We had dinner plans for our cousin's birthday that weekend and I was dreading it. I was feeling upset because my efforts to resolve the situation so far had failed. Fortunately, the night before, I had a ticket to see the Rolling Stones with my friend Samuel.

The concert was in New Jersey, requiring an almost two-hour drive to MetLife Stadium. During the car ride, we mostly discussed the current state of our favorite baseball team, the New York Yankees. I didn't want to ruin the positive vibe by discussing my wife and sister's secret battle, so I kept it bubbling inside my head.

After battling the crowd, we found our seats. We had coffee, made small talk, and kept it light. The noise and the expectation of seeing the Stones live took over.

The audience included spectators of all ages, from my generation to those who weren't even born when the Stones first started. The opening act, a blues singer, sang as his backup band helped lift his sound into the stands. It softened my feelings, but my family issues still lingered in my mind. *I wish I could forget this twisted family problem.*

The stage cleared; the backstage crew swept and prepared for the four dudes refuse to 'grow old when the lights go up.' Suddenly, the stadium went dark. Red lights illuminated the stage into a bright red field of evil and delight. Then, the opening chords of 'Start Me Up', hammered by Keith Richards and Ronnie Wood, exploded through the stadium. Without a moment to realize it, Mick Jagger strode out from the red shadows, singing with the force of an unstoppable hurricane.

Within seconds, I was a kid in 1960s Brooklyn again. My head was clear, and for a short time, I was able to put aside the problems between my wife and my sister. I stomped my feet along to the power of the lyrics and rhythmic sounds of my all-time favorite band.

Music has been a constant companion in my life, a love that has shaped my experiences since childhood. It still has a magical effect, changing my emotional mood with its messages and ability to turn my emotions into sound. It's a connection that transcends age.

HOW MUSIC MAKES US SMARTER

Growing up, we had a hi-fi record player in our Brooklyn home, as well as many records. The music varied from traditional Neapolitan folk songs to Elvis Presley. When my sister became a teenager, Frank Sinatra joined the playlist.

I was too young to have a record collection at that stage. However, I listened and developed a growing love and interest in the melodies I heard. After I saw the Beatles on television, the musical part of my brain wanted more.

I've already talked about how that performance motivated me to begin guitar lessons and join a band throughout my teen years. It was a challenge, but I did it. Taking classes and playing in a band improved my playing and understanding of music theory.

Even in my encore years, I still rock. I take lessons at a music school and play in a neighborhood band. Besides playing more complex music, I realized that music has also helped me remember intricate details, recall complex musical patterns, and support my need to keep learning.

So I have a somewhat unusual suggestion that you might find intriguing or even crazy: now that you've got some free time, why not learn to play an instrument? It requires overcoming fear and getting off the couch, but you will find it easier than you think.

How do you select the instrument? First, think about your favorite type of music. Next, use Google to search for performers who play that type of music. Read all the information, maybe listen to some of your favorite songs, and refresh your memory about what you love about the musicians. Ask yourself these questions: [8-9, 13, 16]

1. Who was your favorite musician? Why?

2. What song(s) did they play?

3. What song do you like the best? Why?

4. What instrument(s) did they play?

5. What instrument do you want to try learning? Why?

I can hear your thoughts as you consider this seemingly enormous task: "This guy is crazy?" "I don't have any talent." "I don't have the time to learn something."[11]

These are all legitimate excuses but they are also simply ways to remain on the couch. Now is the time for us as older adults because there's no getting it back once time passes. So, go for it. You may be surprised at the results, as many cognitive benefits can come from learning a new instrument. Increasing mental stimulation can help delay cognitive decline, potentially preventing the onset of Alzheimer's. You may experience improvement in focus and productivity for everyday activities outside of music as well. For example, there may be a significant improvement in memory and recall for reading, monitoring bank accounts, and correctly managing medication schedules. Also, playing an instrument helps improve coordination, motor control, and dexterity. [2, 5- 10, 12-13, 16]

Music activates parts of the brain responsible for memory and language (temporal lobes), emotions (amygdala and limbic system), and motor coordination (cerebellum and basal ganglia). Continued brain activity strengthens neural connections, creating a cognitive reserve that slows memory decline and enhances critical thinking. [2, 6, 8, 16]

You'll also notice a pronounced improvement in fine motor skills and dexterity and find yourself recognizing patterns and using them to play more challenging songs. [2, 9-10, 12, 16]

HOW MUSIC MAKES US HAPPIER

Music is far more accessible today than it used to be. Many music streaming services are easily available, such as Spotify or Apple Music. You can also purchase headphones or earbuds, including wireless ones, to listen as you walk or complete chores.

The emotional benefits of listening to music are also apparent. It has been shown to lessen stress and anxiety as well as trigger and enhance memories. For example, imagine listening to a song that you heard during your high school prom. As you listen, the memories of the dance all come rushing in: the butterflies you got around your first romantic crush, or how happy you were dancing with your friends, or having a deep conversation with your favorite teacher. These memories can change moods, release negative emotions, and lessen feelings of isolation, as it did for me when I recently went to see The Rolling Stones with Samuel. [2, 6, 8-10, 12-13, 16]

It helps us express our emotions and let go of negative feelings. It makes us more aware of ourselves and our environment, promoting mindfulness. It can make us feel less alone too, especially when the lyrics or melody expresses our certain emotional or life experiences: we realize others are feeling the same way. [1, 2, 8,]

It's a way to get our imaginations going as we listen to it. Think of what comes to mind when you hear John Lennon's 'Imagine'. It also increases social connections when you play or hear music with others.[9] It can even become an intergenerational activity. For example, my 16-year-old niece enjoys examining the cover art of my vinyl records from the 60s.

HOW THE VISUAL ARTS MAKE US SMARTER

COGNITIVE BENEFITS OF THE VISUAL ARTS

This chapter will refer to the visual arts as two distinct experiences. The first is to **view paintings** at a museum or gallery. The second is **creating art** for yourself, at home or in a community setting.

AT THE MUSEUM

Let's pretend we are at New York's Museum of Modern Art (MOMA) looking at Van Gogh's *The Starry Night*. What skills do we need to understand what we're looking at? [6, 8, 10]

- **Visual and analytical skills** to interpret Van Gogh's use of color, texture, and dizzying composition.

- **Memory recall** from our art appreciation classes or previous viewing of this painting – for example, long lectures in college or our first viewing of this painting, in person or from a picture.

- **Creating a narrative** that assigns meaning to what we see – where did those stars come from?

- **Revise your explanation** based on your ability to reflect on your thinking and conclusions.

HOW CREATING ART MAKES US SMARTER AND HAPPIER

Creating art can involve various activities such as painting, drawing, collages, sewing, or pottery. All forms of art require continuous focus and attention to important details. After identifying these details, the artist must choose the colors, materials, techniques, size, and form of the artwork. After making these decisions, the creator must identify and follow the steps to complete the piece. [2, 6, 8-10,]

Equally important, the artist has to adapt to the workspace and materials available. For example, if the workspace is small, then instead of using an easel, the artist must draw or paint on any flat surface available. If there is a shortage of supplies, the artist may use only a limited variety of materials. [2, 6, 8-10,]

Finally, the artist has to express their abstract ideas and emotions in a concrete form, illustrating the theme or concept of their work. It requires compassion and creative thinking that the artist has developed over the years. [2, 6]

When older adults engage in the creative process, they simulate the same process artists undertake in their creative pursuit, in expressing their innermost thoughts and feelings. It enables them to express themselves through a different medium and promotes cognitive stimulation and growth. [2, 6]

The creative process also supports the emotional wellbeing of older adults. While engaged in art projects, they develop a sense of purpose, find new ways to express themselves, and often connect to fellow art explorers. The activity reduces stress, boosts self-esteem, encourages exploration, and promotes lifelong learning. [2, 4, 6, 8, 12]

TIPS TO INTEGRATE MUSIC AND THE VISUAL ARTS INTO OUR DAILY LIVES

MUSIC

Technology makes listening to music accessible to older adults twenty-four hours a day. Spotify, Apple Music, and Pandora are music streaming services that are readily available on many devices, such as smartphones, tablets, and computers. You can create playlists to suit your needs. For example, you can listen to morning music to start and energize your body and mind, or afternoon music to help maintain your focus and energy. [2, 13, 16]

When used carefully and in moderation, headphones and earbuds allow you to complete chores while cleaning, gardening, walking, or grocery shopping. The sound of your favorite songs makes these activities feel less burdensome. [2, 13, 16]

To comfort myself, I've created a playlist of my favorite music from the British Invasion of the 1960s, when British bands like The Beatles and The Rolling Stones changed music. This music is not only nostalgic but also helps enrich my day.

Music can also be an active part of life. One can sing in a community group or with family during a karaoke night, dance in Zumba exercise classes, or learn a new instrument. Hospitals and care facilities offer these therapies, and trained therapists guide patients to focus on mental and physical problems such as memory loss, dementia, and issues with movement and balance. The sessions use music and movement to help improve mood, physical health, cognitive stimulation, social connection, and promote social interaction for its participants. [2-3, 5-8, 10, 14, 16]

Live performances can offer powerful experiences that bring music to life. Watching performers sing or play an instrument creates an emotional connection that allows you to release pent-up emotions or stress. Not only do you understand their message but you also feel what they feel. It's a magical connection that takes us to another level of understanding. [6, 8, 13]

Music can be a great way to spark conversations with others, even grandchildren or younger family members. Recently, my nieces and I explored my vinyl record collection, discussing the cover designs, printed lyrics, and song meanings. We spent a considerable amount of time discussing the Beatles' Sgt. Pepper's Lonely Hearts Band record jacket and identifying the cardboard cutouts of Bob Dylan, Marilyn Monroe, Mae West, and Albert Einstein.

Engaging in art is also critical for us as we age. Taking art classes at local centers, religious institutions, or schools is one way of learning to sketch, draw, and paint. Visiting museums, galleries, and exhibitions can inspire you and expose you to many different art forms. Many museums have websites that allow you to explore art from different countries. Notable examples include the Louvre and the Musée d'Orsay in Paris, the British Museum in London, the Tokyo Metropolitan Museum of Art, and the Rijksmuseum in Amsterdam. [6, 8, 10]

It can be beneficial to set up a cozy space at home where you create illustrations, drawings, or paint images. While engaged in this work, you can listen to music and combine the benefits of both activities. [8]

You could also combine both art and writing in a coloring journal. As you write your thoughts and feelings, you can illustrate or draw your interpretation of the entry, expressing yourself through another medium. [2]

A SPECIAL CONCLUSION – ODE TO A MUSIC TEACHER

I informally interviewed my former guitar teacher for my conclusion to this chapter. I wanted to present and summarize his feelings about music and his history around it. He is a young, talented musician who effortlessly switches between playing the drums and playing rock guitar.

He grew up in a small Massachusetts town with not much to do, so he had a lot of unused energy. Luckily, his mom and brother were heavy into music, so he naturally developed a strong taste for it. His pent-up energy led him to the drums. When he wasn't skateboarding, he played the drums while listening to metal bands.

As a teenager, he became so talented that he joined his brother's band and played alongside them. Whenever his mom was home, the sounds of her diverse vinyl collection filled the air, shaping his music education.

He continued playing drums and guitar during college. After college, he focused on music and did well. However, the music scene took a toll on him, and he turned to alcohol and any other comforting tool he could find.

But when music filled his ears, drowning out the world's noise, it brought him solace. He discovered that playing drums or guitar could resuscitate his temporary detour from making music.

For him, melodies, beats, or tunes are the fluids that rush through his veins. When he plays an instrument, he disappears into another realm of being and peace. He becomes the foundation and propels his metal band into a sound that breaks heavy metal barriers.

Exploring visual arts and music will add purpose to your life and reveal a hidden part of your soul. Watching my teacher perform is proof of this revitalization and transformation.

Music has a similar effect on me. Whenever I sense myself slipping into a sad or depressive mood, my guitar and music help me fight against that descent into darkness. Holding a guitar pick and playing along with a backing track, I chase away that mood by strumming the chords and notes of a song from the British Invasion that I mentioned earlier. After playing several songs, I feel like myself again and am ready to write the next page.

CHAPTER 14

ADAPTATION IS OUR SILVER LINING

Aging is not lost youth but a new stage of opportunity and strength.

Betty Friedan

I worked my butt off for over 50 years. I always kept a routine and followed a straight path, leading to burnout. You can conclude that I lived the life of a monk.

As I crept into my late 60s, a particular incident shook me from this paralysis. It was a regular fall evening, and I played a Rolling Stone song on my Strat – 'Gimme Shelter'.

As I finished, I heard my thoughtful neighbor applauding my efforts. It was wild because I had never heard her clap her hands before. This unexpected act of appreciation was the jolt I needed to realize that I was not living my life to the fullest.

"Thanks so much!" I yelled back.

"No problem," she responded. "Keep it flowing." I did.

Later, at my desk, with the sun disappearing for the day, I journaled about the satisfaction I felt when I heard her applause. As I wrote, the subject shifted to the current state of my life. If

I remember correctly, I described it as lifeless, like 'living in a corpse', and feeling stuck. It took me several days to admit I had to change. I always hated and feared change.

With the guidance of my therapist and several self-improvement books, I started overcoming ingrained behaviors and beliefs. This work helped me understand why I found change difficult and provided practical strategies.

In this chapter, I will identify the practices and approaches I used to make change possible. While I still have more work to do, I am committed to it. As we age, we will face new challenges that require the skills we've developed in our careers, such as resilience, adaptability, perseverance, critical thinking, communication, and a commitment to continuous learning. By using these skills, we can create a fulfilling life during our later years and adapt as needed. [5, 11, 14]

In her article 'Age and the Potential to Change', Jeanette Leardi explains that older adults can adapt and change while remaining determined to maintain their lifestyles as they age. She also asserts that older adults possess greater brain capacity and have sophisticated methods for interpreting and applying information. She notes that older adults can adjust their perceptions and behaviors even with cognitive impairment, as long as they are in a supportive care environment. [11]

STRESS FACTORS FOR OLDER ADULTS FACE

Older adults encounter financial difficulties, challenges in accessing quality healthcare, and both cognitive and physical decline. If society does not assist them in coping with and adapting to these stress factors, their remaining years will be challenging. [5-6, 8, 13, 15]

Changes in living conditions can occur as people reach retirement age. As mentioned earlier, this transition may involve moving to an assisted living facility or dealing with feelings of loneliness and boredom while aging at home. In these situations, it is common for individuals to experience stress as they adjust to their new circumstances. [6, 8, 11, 13, 15]

Health issues impact older adults, particularly heart disease, mobility issues, impaired vision, hearing loss, osteoporosis, and arthritis. A shortage of healthcare providers and insurance difficulties worsens these challenges. [2-3, 6, 8-9, 13, 15]

Loss of purpose, which often occurs after retirement and leaving a steady job and daily schedule, can lead to isolation, depression, decreased confidence, cognitive decline, poor health, increased stress vulnerability, and a shorter life expectancy. [6, 8, 13, 15]

Money management problems often stem from insufficient retirement savings, rising healthcare costs, limited financial literacy, and challenges in adapting to life without a regular paycheck. These issues can lead to emotional distress, stress, uncertainty, feelings of failure, self-blame, and family tension. [5-6, 17]

Transportation is vital for older adults to access medical care, shopping, and social activities. For those who have driven for years, being told to 'hand over the keys' can diminish their sense of identity and independence. This also places added pressure on caregivers and family members who assist them. [5, 8, 11, 13,]

Losses such as that of a spouse, friends, or neighbors can deeply affect older adults, similar to biological changes. These events often lead to depression, decreased security, emotional difficulties, and a deep sense of emptiness. [8, 11, 15]

THE EFFECTS OF COGNITIVE AND PHYSICAL DECLINE ON PROCESSING CHANGE

Both our cognitive and physical abilities are, unfortunately, inevitable. They can occur either at a fast or slow rate. Regular exercise, a healthy diet, and preventive medicine can slow these changes. Despite these measures, they will still occur as we age. [2-3, 8, 11, 15]

Older adults experience a multitude of cognitive issues as they age. They may process information more slowly, struggle with focus and multitasking, and find it harder to plan and finish daily tasks. They also may forget names, lose words in conversations, and have difficulty processing and remembering information. Unfortunately, they undergo significant changes in their spatial awareness, making it challenging to drive or even take a leisurely walk in the neighborhood. [2, 6,11-12, 13, 15]

Older adults often worry about losing their independence, including the ability to make decisions, drive, bathe, or cook for themselves. They also fear having to move to a communal setting (as opposed to choosing it for themselves) where they would share a room, meals, and take part in group activities. These fears can negatively affect their health, resilience, and emotional well-being. [8, 11, 15]

Technology can empower older adults by facilitating social connections through smartphones and social media, managing healthcare via telemedicine, and enabling online banking and shopping. However, it also poses challenges, such as the need to learn new systems amid rapid changes, risks of scams and privacy concerns, and limitations faced by those with vision impairments, hearing loss, and mobility issues. [13, 15, 17]

These changes, along with the realization that their quality of life has decreased, can affect their emotional health. Many individuals experience increased anxiety, depression, and a sense of loss of independence, resulting in feelings of isolation and marginalization. [2, 6, 11-13, 15]

Older adults experience physical decline as they age, which includes reduced mobility and balance issues, impaired vision, hearing, taste and smell. They may also develop arthritis, osteoporosis, and are more susceptible to heart disease, diabetes, and high blood pressure. Many older individuals suffer from other common conditions, such as cataracts, back and neck pain, and chronic obstructive pulmonary disease (COPD), which can make it difficult to breathe. [3, 15]

Of course, we must still persevere, accept, and adapt to these challenges, which require the skills we have developed through our lives. [8, 9]

ADAPTING TO CHANGE FOR OLDER ADULTS

Several weeks ago, amid the heat of NYC in July, I spotted an older adult gazing at her painting canvas in a local park. At first, I didn't want to disturb her. She appeared to be in a creative trance, searching for an elusive detail.

After waiting for a few moments, and with my coffee cup in hand, I approached her with an appreciative smile. It must have been the nose of my Yoka sneakers on the dry grass; she turned and looked at me.

"Can I help you, sir?" she asked.

"Sorry to disturb you," I began nervously. "I couldn't help seeing that you were painting using watercolors."

She nodded.

"I'm sorry I disrupted your painting," I added.

"It's fine. My husband does it all the time," she smiled.

I continued. "It appears you are painting the trees by the fence opposite the street. It's really good and so realistic!"

"I didn't think anyone would recognize it."

"Seriously? It's perfect."

Her smile grew warmer. "Again, thanks for your interest. I took classes at the local community center for six months. I love it."

"Only six months?"

"Yes. As a retired nurse, I needed something to help transition from stressful, long days at my hospital. I didn't think I could do it, but here I am. And loving it."

Before I left, the retired nurse confessed she was 75 years old. I spotted her several more times, and each time she was completing another painting of the park's scenic landscape. In the following instances, I waved to her, and she reciprocated with the smile of an accomplished painter.

This painter is an example of an older adult who has begun her journey into her encore years by accepting and adapting to her circumstances.

My research on adaptation and my own experiences have provided strategies to facilitate adaptation as we age. Adaptation is more than survival; it means flourishing when life gets hard. [1, 3, 8, 10-12]

Adapting begins with drawing on life experiences – our resilience and perseverance reserves. It's remembering the advice of the philosopher Friedrich Nietzsche: "What doesn't kill you makes you stronger." [9, 16]

It starts with discovering a purpose, much like the painter described above. Embracing a purpose offers direction and motivation for growth. It makes you optimistic and ready for your challenges as you age. [5, 9, 11-12, 15]

Emotional wellbeing allows you to develop a positive outlook and choose hope over despair. Leardi's research suggests that a positive mindset leads to self-compassion, allowing us to appreciate who we are and what we have while defeating negative self-talk. [1, 9, 14]

This positive mindset and willingness to adapt ensure that we remain curious. This curiosity will help us engage in activities like reading books, art, sketching, gardening, or learning how to play an instrument. [1, 9, 11-12, 15]

A sense of fulfillment will enable us to stay active, eat healthy, exercise, and focus on preventive medicine instead of curative or reactive medicine. [8-9, 11, 15]

Some of the other benefits of our ability to adapt are better relationships with family and friends, limited cognitive decline, recognizing this period as one of discovery rather than decline, and attempts to use technology. [8-9, 11-13, 15]

BEHAVIORS AND BELIEFS THAT SUPPORT CHANGE AND ADAPTATION

Adaptation is a natural part of aging. I remember my first day teaching middle school English, when my students overwhelmed me. With the help of an assistant principal, I gained control over my classes. It required careful reflection, a desire to learn, and a purpose: to teach and succeed.

You might have had similar situations in your career where a project, a demanding job, or even a person presented a problem. It required immediate attention, a change in strategy, and belief in yourself.

As older adults, the challenges we encounter and the solutions we implement now significantly affect how we live for the rest of our lives. To ensure that aging becomes a journey of new beginnings rather than one filled with despair and regret, we must adopt activities that provide a consistent source of purpose and self-reward. Dr. Kado suggests, "Having something meaningful on the calendar can literally add days to your life." [5, 9]

Refrain from keeping feelings in by seeking professional help or expressing them through the arts. Online services offer counseling and emotional support. You can find one in your location by simply searching online or asking your primary caregiver for recommendations. [6, 8-9]

Keep a sense of curiosity about life and living. Do it if you have always wanted to ride a horse, plant a community garden, or travel. It will energize you and open your eyes to other possibilities. [1, 9, 11-12]

Read, visit museums (in-person or online), listen to music, and learn to dance. These activities exercise your mind and help you discover the inner strength needed to adapt and overcome unexpected challenges.

Accept new limitations and accommodate them by finding acceptable alternatives. If you keep a journal, you might find it hard to write 500 words daily like you used to. That's okay – find a realistic word count that fits your current focus and skill level and make it part of your routine. [9, 14]

Another example might be at the gym. Don't compare your push-up ability to someone much younger or fitter. Focus on what *you* can do, or ask a trainer for advice.

Exercise, get enough sleep, eat well, and share your gifts with others. Research shows that your emotional health will improve if you feel physically well. Take the time to volunteer at a community organization or to talk to your grandchildren about your life experiences. Sharing your insights and knowledge will bring you a sense of fulfillment and a more profound sense of giving back. [6, 8-9, 13]

Learn to fight negative self-talk. Listening to it could impact your motivation to explore, increase anxiety or depression, cause a loss of a sense of purpose, increase dependence, and affect your emotional and physical health. [9, 14] When I hear my inner critic saying, "I am a lousy writer," I affirm, "Each day I write, I help others."

Attempt to maintain your friendships with the people you know and love. Use technology to stay in touch or plan periodic meetings for breakfast or lunch. Make new friends by participating in community center activities, book clubs, or neighborhood events. [6, 8, 11-15, 17]

Savor life's magical moments as they occur. You know the old saying, "Stop and smell the roses." If you are walking in your neighborhood and spot flowers blooming on the first day of spring, take a moment to enjoy this miracle of nature. Or you see a mother and child in a grocery store, stop shopping and soak in the feelings of tenderness and joy that the moment represents. [9]

Finally, appreciate what you have; don't dwell on what you lack. This positive mindset will enhance your ability to accept yourself and allow you to explore new opportunities. [1-2, 6, 9, 14-15]

CONCLUSION

My research for this chapter suggests that changing your fundamental nature is impossible. However, we can embrace a silver lining. It's learning to adapt. Adapting doesn't erase challenges but transforms them into opportunities for growth and purpose. Life throws obstacles; we can't stop this unforeseen barrage, but we can control how we respond to them as we age. It demands the resilience, knowledge, and experience we have gained. [2, 4-6, 8-9, 11-13, 15]

I believe that is not simply about living longer but improving the quality of the years we have. Put all that anguish and despair behind you. Start anew. Think about what you now have time to pursue that you previously put aside. Change any defeatist, negative self-talk. Make it instead a driving force for change. Then, pursue those goals with the same passion you had earlier in life. It requires finding the silver lining that the power of adaptation offers. I assure you that your efforts will help you realize the dreams you once put aside in order to earn a living. You can still become a painter, a traveler, an entrepreneur, or an expert gardener. It involves tapping into the inner strength you already possess.

CHAPTER 15

AN ENCORE

People often compare New York City bus rides to a theater on wheels. You have diverse characters, constantly changing scenes, surprising drama and comedy, entertaining dialogue, masterful dance moves, and a shared experience.

But one late June morning, my journey was more than an ordinary bumpy ride. Strangely, I only had to wait five minutes for the bus instead of the usual twenty. After paying my fare, I looked for a seat in the front section reserved for older adults or individuals with disabilities.

Despite the challenges, the resilience of the older adults on the bus was inspiring. A woman in a wheelchair, secured to the wall by carefully positioned straps, blocked my path to the seat. As the bus pulled out of the stop, I stepped over the bottom of the wheelchair and plopped into a hard-surfaced seat.

When I looked up, I noticed her eyes were closed, and her hands rested on her lap. She was alone, without a healthcare attendant. Within a New York minute, the bus pulled into the next stop. First, a young woman entered, paid her fare, and brazenly pushed two enormous suitcases to the first seat she spotted.

As she sat down, I wanted to tell her they were seats for older adults or the infirm. But when I saw her puzzled and angry expression, I kept quiet.

I looked up and watched a dapper man, about 90, with a cane, enter the bus. His hand trembled as he paid his fare. He, with great effort, turned to his left. He spotted the empty seat right next to me.

Even though I had trouble with my own balance, I could see that he needed my help. Since no one else moved, I got up. I placed my arms around his lower back and guided him to his seat. "Thank you, sir," he whispered. I just nodded and smiled.

Once he sat down, passengers gingerly passed through our special section. But the drama wasn't over yet. A nanny with a baby stroller entered. *Oh, shit,* I thought to myself. *How will she get that stroller past the wheelchair and the luggage piled in the aisle?*

Somehow, the lady in the wheelchair came to life. "Damn it! I gotta get off at the next stop. You're blocking me."

"Relax, lady," the nanny responded calmly. "I'll make it work."

"You better."

After two traffic lights, we reached the stop. The bus driver left his partition and released the wheelchair from the protective straps. He then returned to his spot and lowered the ramp from the bus to the curb.

The nanny exited the bus, pushing the stroller down the ramp. Next came the lady in the wheelchair, who muttered "Thank Jesus," as she also left the bus.

I wish I could say it ended there. This is New York, and nothing is easy. Five minutes later, in the middle of the city, another wheelchair user entered with two more aged adults. The problem was that the two seats once occupied by the wheelchair had now been taken by two aged customers.

The tireless driver asked them to vacate their seats. As they followed his instruction, I heard one of them mumble, "This is crazy. We should have left later."

The wheelchair, with a well-dressed woman sitting in it, waited to be strapped in. Her two friends joined the others standing in the aisle. The bus driver completed the process for the second time.

I returned to my book and held my breath. Luckily, I only had two more stops before I could escape. Once I did, I headed to a coffee shop for a much-needed break and caffeine.

I could have started the book with this bus ride. I chose to place it here for several reasons. First, the incidents described would have passed off as a typical day here. I wouldn't have been sensitive to the issues of ageism and ableism, the invisibility of older adults in our society, and the difficulty of the sick and older adults experiencing access to safe transportation. [3, 5]

Second, I wanted to reinforce the need for us to take action. At this point in my life, it is futile to wait for politicians to address the living, medical, and emotional needs of older adults.[1,5]

My motivation for helping on the bus was simple: I hated seeing others struggle. I felt a powerful urge to assist without even thinking about it. In both cases, I helped older adults, whom I refer to as 'age colleagues.' Their challenges are common issues, and public transportation presents many obstacles for them. [1, 5]

We need to advocate for changes such as non-slip flooring, priority seating near entrances, step-free access such as ramps, extended boarding times, large-print maps, and audio-visual stop announcements [1, 5, 7]

I have been in my encore years for a few years now. It's been bumpy sometimes. Depression has been part of my life for many years. Despite medication and monthly therapy sessions, it still creeps up on me.

Sometimes I miss my working life and my youth – this can trigger my depression occasionally. Its duration is short-lived, but it still hurts. So I turn to the techniques outlined in this book. [2]

I prioritize my passions and continue to chase them. Writing has become the dominant part of each day. [6, 9, 14] I schedule three hours a day during the week. Reading supports the development of my craft. As I read, I note the author's use of dialogue, the reliance on descriptive phrases, and the format of presenting information.

I stay connected with my family and friends through activities like playing in our band and catching up with fellow gym members. As I mentioned before, I was single until I turned 71. The best part of my day is spending evenings watching movies or cooking shows with my wife and talking to her about them. [15]

Music have always been essential to my life. Since starting my encore years, I've had more time for guitar lessons, and my guitar playing and understanding of harmony and melody have improved. And whenever I feel down, I increase my listening time. The classic rock I grew up with is like Tylenol for my mild depression. It quiets the active turbulence in my head. [2-3]

Regular exercise and medication have enabled me to manage the effects of my auto-immune disease (CIDP – chronic inflammatory demyelinating polyneuropathy). This condition affects my balance, causes muscle weakness, leads to loss of reflexes, results in fatigue, and makes dressing difficult.

My trainer has designed a functional training program that emphasizes building strength and coordination through movements that simulate everyday activities such as walking, climbing stairs, and carrying groceries. These exercises have improved my muscle tone and posture, as well as boosted my self-confidence. [2-3]

We implement the Danish concept of *hygge* (pronounced 'hoo-gah') in our tiny New York City apartment. To combat the city's rampant noise and abnormal confusion, we use soft lighting, a cozy sofa, scented candles, and watch films that highlight the elegance of nature and the simple pleasures of life. [2]

BOOKENDS

Simon and Garfunkel wrote a song called 'Bookends' which portrays two older male friends sitting on a park bench like bookends. I used to think it was sad: it's sunset, and they seem isolated and waiting for the end.

I listened to it again, and now the message feels quite different. The men are two older adults who have successfully navigated life after many years of work. They are now content to rest and contemplate what comes next.

I have known two older men in my life who remind me of the two sitting on the bench. The first I will call Doc, and the second Mr. Joe.

As his nickname suggests, Doc was a doctor at a local hospital. He is in his eighties. I first met Doc a few years ago at my gym.

He was pumping iron, doing bicep curls with a 20-pound barbell, followed by hammer curls with ten-pound dumbbells.

We finished our workouts and headed to the locker room for our much-needed showers. After dressing, I saw him sitting in the gym's lounge area. I sat beside him and introduced myself, mentioning that I was impressed by his workout routine.

"Nice to meet you," he said. "I noticed you too. You're pretty good yourself. But you take too much time between your exercises. You've got to move to pick up your heart rate." He then smiled at me. "The name's Jacob Wilson. My friends call me Doc."

"Hi, Doc. You're right. But I get tired quickly and have to catch my breath." I then looked at him, waiting for more advice.

"Are you getting enough rest? What's your diet like?" He looked straight at me.

"I get enough sleep. But I don't eat well," I admitted.

He took out a pen and paper from his knapsack. "Richard, right? Let me write down some simple suggestions for you, for sleeping longer and eating better."

After our conversation, I took his advice, and from that day we became gym buddies, occasionally catching up over coffee at an Italian cafe. I learned he had spent over 50 years as a cancer specialist and researcher. He also volunteered twice weekly at his hospital's research library. Our time together has improved my health and made my emotional outlook on retirement more positive and purposeful.

Today, Doc is still lifting weights and observing me, so I continue my workout routine with minimal rest. He is part of my journey to becoming a certified gym rat and my inspiration to write this second book.

The second person, whom I call Mr. Joe, was my father. His parents came to Ellis Island from Naples, Italy, in 1910. He was born in Brooklyn in 1914 and left school after the third grade. He helped his father cut lawns and complete basic repairs in homes nestled in middle-class neighborhoods.

He married my mom, they had me and my sister, and we lived in many rental apartments throughout my childhood.

Mr. Joe always dreamed of having a house with a lawn and a place to erect a statue of his Blessed Mother, Mary. He worked a lot of different jobs throughout his life, with hopes of achieving this dream. Three years before he retired, he bought his first house. He was 62 years old.

During high school, college, and my first teaching job, I had the privilege of talking to him while we sat in his glorious garden. The discussions ranged from school problems to career choices to girls.

The guiding principle that he taught me, that has shaped my life, is, "Richard, work hard no matter where you are." My father exemplified this belief, working steadily for over 60 years despite his limited education, the Great Depression, and World War II. He ensured that my sister and I received an excellent education and had the chance to succeed.

Next, he wanted us to not only think of ourselves, and to consider others' needs as well. This belief stemmed from his Catholic faith. He was active in church events and assisted the priests in their pastoral duties. For example, he helped them raise money with yearly bazaars and fundraiser events, sold refreshments at our baseball games, and ran the weekly bingo nights.

Finally, he advocated the importance of family in everyday life. Mr. Joe was the patriarch of our extended family. He arranged for all my aunts, cousins, and friends to meet at least twice a year to remember our deceased family members. We would attend Mass, eat an enormous dinner in my parents' basement, and listen to Italian cultural music from Naples or Calabria.

Now that I am the oldest member of my extended family, I, along with my wife, organize our large family gatherings for the holidays. While sitting at our celebratory dinners, I often think of Mr. Joe – eating, watching his guests, and smiling. Like him and Doc, I feel a sense of purpose and happiness as I navigate my life while growing older.

Like the two men portrayed in the song 'Bookends', I imagine Doc, Mr. Joe, and I sitting together on a bench. We're by the tranquil River Arno in Florence, Italy. No words are needed; our peaceful smiles say it all. Despite struggles and setbacks, we have found purpose, dignity, and laughter in our encore years. We know that more awaits us, wherever we choose to go next.

GLOSSARY

The following glossary defines key concepts discussed throughout *The Encore Years*. Each term highlights themes of aging, purpose, creativity, and well-being.

A

Adaptability: The ability to adjust your behavior, emotions, or goals based on the present circumstances or events in your life. [3]

Ageism: The prejudicial belief that older adults are in decline and incapable of living a purpose-driven life. [1,3]

Aging in Place: Occurs when older adults choose to age in their own homes instead of a retirement community. [1,3] *See also Retirement Communities.*

C

Continuous Learning: Older adults who continue to explore and learn new ideas or engage in hobbies or passions they neglected earlier in life because of family or careers. [3] *See also Neuroplasticity.*

D

Digital Divide: The gap between people without access to computers, smartphones, and the internet. [12] *See also Continuous Learning.*

E

Elder Speak: An example of ageism occurs when a younger person speaks to an older adult using overly simplified and condescending language, often in a loud voice, because they assume the older adult cannot understand them. This can include using terms like 'potty,' 'boo-boo,' or 'nap time' to refer to adult activities, or addressing the person as 'sweetie,' 'dear,' or 'honey' instead of using their name. [10] *See also Ageism.*

Encore Years: These are the years or time we have after our working days end. Some people refer to them as their golden or retirement years. [5, 6] *See also Purposeful Aging.*

F

Fixed Mindset: Occurs when someone refuses to change a belief or opinion despite the evidence or truth. [10]

G

Growth Mindset: Occurs when someone adapts their beliefs about an idea, explores new passions, and engages in continuous learning. [10]

H

Hidden Sugars: Food companies often disguise sugars or sweeteners in our foods by adding them under different names, such as sucrose, high-fructose corn syrup, glucose, or dextrose. Hidden sugars are often present in processed foods, sauces, cereals, and beverages advertised as 'natural' or 'healthy.' [10]

I

Inspiration Porn: This occurs when a younger person sees an older adult lifting weights, playing chess, gardening, or sketching, and asks, "How old are you? I can't believe it." This question reflects the assumption that aging means decline, rather than a continued fulfilling life. [1] *See also Ageism.*

Intergenerational Connections: Occur when older adults engage with younger individuals, such as an older volunteer tutoring third graders. [4]

L

Loss of Purpose: Older adults who retire and remain inactive – like spending their retirement on an extended vacation – can miss out on meaningful pursuits. This inaction may lead to isolation, depression, decreased confidence, memory loss, reduced independence, and a shorter life expectancy. [1,6]

M

Metabolism: The process by which the body converts food and drink into energy. As we age, our bodies burn calories more slowly than they used to. This makes it easier to gain weight and lose muscle mass. [2] *See also Resilience.*

Mindfulness: Mindfulness is a practice that encourages calm and focus on the present moment without judgment. Techniques like gentle breathing, movement, or quiet reflection can reduce stress and improve overall well-being. [8,11]

N

Neuroplasticity: The brain has a natural ability to adapt, change, and grow as we age, especially when we engage in activities that promote continuous learning. Examples of such activities include learning to sketch, writing daily, joining book clubs, volunteering, and exploring new technology. [3,10] *See also Continuous Learning.*

Negative Self-Talk: The voice in our heads that tells us negative things about ourselves, like "I'm too old to learn to paint," "I'm a burden to my family," or "My best years are behind me." [9]

P

Passion: The state of being fully immersed in an activity, where time seems to disappear. It captivates your attention and brings energy, joy, and purpose. Shared passions include writing, music, exercise, travel, gardening, and enjoying movies or ballet. [6] *See also Continuous Learning*

Purposeful Aging: Refers to the process in which older adults cultivate a meaningful life after retirement by exploring new and existing interests. For instance, they might take continuing education courses in subjects like art history or computer skills, join a book or discussion club, or even start a garden. [4,5] *See also Encore Years and Loss of Purpose.*

Preventive Care: Proactively maintaining health through regular checkups, screenings, and vaccinations helps detect issues like high blood pressure, diabetes, or cancer early, allowing for timely treatment. It also involves maintaining a healthy lifestyle by eating well, exercising, and staying socially active. [10]

R

Retirement Communities: Locations that help older adults age safely and independently often offer private apartments, communal dining, recreational activities, and optional services like housekeeping, transportation, and fitness programs. [1,7]

Resilience: The ability to stay strong and move on despite setbacks like health challenges, loss of a spouse or friend, financial changes, loss of independence, or a change in one's living conditions. [3,8]

S

Social Isolation: Occurs when older adults stop interacting with other people. Potential causes are retirement, losing a spouse or close friends, health issues, or limited mobility, making it challenging to stay socially active. [10, 13]

T

Third Act: The life we lead after our working years is an opportunity to live purposefully by embracing new possibilities, whether through volunteering, learning, traveling, or pursuing creative goals. [5, 6] *See also Encore Years.*

W

Wellness: Involves paying attention to life's physical, mental, emotional, and social aspects. It requires making conscious daily choices, such as selecting nutritious foods, exercising regularly, staying connected with others, managing stress, and engaging in daily activities that provide satisfaction and meaning. [2, 4, 10]

ENDNOTES

CHAPTER 1: A HISTORY OF AGEISM

1. Applewhite, A. (2000). *This Chair Rocks: A Manifesto Against Ageism*. New York: Celadon Books.

2. Gendron, T. (2022). *Ageism Unmasked: Exploring Age Bias And How to End It*. New Hampshire: Steerforth Press L.L.C.

3. Levy, B. (2022). *Breaking the Code: How Your Beliefs About Aging Determine How Long & Well You Live*. New York: Harper Collins.

CHAPTER 2 LIFE AFTER WORK: THE ENCORE YEARS

1. Friedman, M. (2007). *Encore: Finding Work That Matters in the Second Half of Life*. Philadelphia: Public Affairs.

2. Friedman, Thomas L. "The Encore Years," *The New York Times*, January 20, 2007.

3. TED. (2011, January 4). *Life's Third Act*. YouTube. https://www.youtube.com/watch?v=IHyR7p6_hn0

CHAPTER 3 MEDICINE AND AGING

1. Applewhite, A. (2000). *This Chair Rocks: A Manifesto Against Ageism*. New York: Celadon Books.

2. Attia, P. (2023). Outlive: Work in Progress: The High Price of Ignoring Emotional Health. In *Outlive: The Science & Art of Longevity* (pp. 377-408). New York: Penguin Random House.

3. Brodmerkel, S., & Barker, R. (2019). Hitting the 'glass wall': Investigating everyday ageism in the advertising industry. The Sociological Review, 67(6), 1383-1399. https://doi.org/10.1177/0038026119837147

4. Gendron, T. (2022). *Ageism Unmasked: Exploring Age Bias and How to End It.* New Hampshire: Steerforth Press.

5. Lachs, M. (2010). *What your doctor won't tell you about getting older: An insider's survival manual for outsmarting the Health-Care System.* New York: Viking Penguin

6. Levy, B. (2022). *Breaking the Code: How Your Beliefs About Aging Determine How Long & Well You Live.* New York: Harper Collins.

7. "What are the statistics for women who are underrepresented in clinical trials for leading diseases? Harvard Medical School reported this in 2022," OpenAI, February 18, 2025.

CHAPTER 4: THE MEDIA AND AGEISM

1. Applewhite, Ashton. *This Chair Rocks: A Manifesto Against Ageism.* New York, New York: Celadon Books, 2016.

2. Benshoff, Harry M., and Sean Griffin. *America on Film: Representing Race, Class, Gender, and Sexuality at the Movies,* 3rd ed. Hoboken, NJ: John Wiley & Sons, Inc., 2021.

3. Mariann Aalda's (2020) TEDx Talk, *Ageism Is A Bully, Stand Up To It.*

4. Choi-Allum, Lona, Farago, F. (2025). Breaking stereotypes, the push for real representation of older adults in movies and television. Retrieved from https://www.aarp.org/pri/topics/social-leisure/activities-interests/ageism-movies-television

5. Collins, L. M. (2019, September 25). Ageism is Costing this Country Billions. Here's How. *Deseret News. AARP* /https://www.deseret.com/indepth/2019/9/24/20880106/elderly-media-portrayal-ageism-us-economy-aarp

6. Dychtwald, K. (2021, September 8). Ageism is Alive and Well in Advertising. *AARP.* Retrieved from www.aarp.org/work/age-discrimination/ageism-in-advertising

7. Edstrom, M. (2018). Visibility Patterns of Gendered Ageism in the Media Buzz: A Study of the representation of Gender and Age Over Three Decades. *Feminist Media Studies* 18(1), 77–93. https://doi.org/10.1080/14680777.2018.1409989

8. Eisenberg, R. (2022). Ageism in Hollywood: The worst I've ever seen it. *Next Avenue.* Retrieved from https://www.nextavenue.org/ageism-in-hollywood-the-worst-ive-ever-seen-it

9. Eisenberg, R. (2023). Ageism in the media: An insider's perspective. *Generations: Society of Aging.* Retrieved from https://generations.asaging.org/ageism-media-insiders-perspective

10. Esposito, Lisa. "Ageism in Top TV Shows May Affect Seniors' Well-Being." *U.S.News.* U.S.News, 2017. https://health.usnews.com/wellness/articles/2017-10-18/ageism-in-top-tv-shows-may-affect-seniors-well-being

11. Gendron, T. (2022). *Ageism Unmasked: Exploring Age Bias And How to End It.* New Hampshire: Steerforth Press L.L.C.

12. Green, C. (2018). TV tropes and ageism: How` kids' pop culture promotes discrimination. Retrieved from https://generations.asaging.org/ageism-media-insiders-perspective

13. Hatch, L. R. (2005). *Gender and ageism.* American Society of Aging. 29, no. 3: Retrieved from https://www.jstor.org/stable/pdf/26555400.pdf?refreqid=fastly-default%3A7ae270efc36a8e4f839cd9be265b5d67&ab_segments=&initiator=recommender&acceptTC=1

14. Hsu, T. (2021). "Older People Are Ignored and Distorted in Ageist Marketing, Report Finds". *New York Times.* Retrieved from 'Fabulous Four Review-Starry Cast Deserves Better in Silly, Simplistic Comedy'. *The Guardian,* July 25, 2024. guardian.com/film/article/2024/jul/25/the-fabulous-four-review-susan-sarandon-bette-midler

15. Kaczmarek, Emilia. "Promoting Diseases to Promote Drugs: The Role of the Pharmaceutical Industry in Fostering Good and Bad Medicalization." *British Pharmacological Society,* March 15, 2021, 34–40. https://doi.org/ 10.1111/bcp.14835

16. Lee, Benjamin. "The Fabulous Four Review--Starry Cast Deserves Better in Silly, Simplistic Comedy." *The Guardian,* July 25, 2024. uardian.com/film/article/2024/jul/25/the-fabulous-four-review-susan-sarandon-bette-midler

17. Levy, B. (2022). *Breaking the Code: How Your Beliefs About Aging Determine How Long & Well You Live.* New York: Harper Collins.

18. Loos, E., Ivan, L. (2018). Visual Ageism in the Media. In: Ayalon, L, Tesch-Romer, C (eds) *Contemporary Perspectives on Ageism. International Perspectives on Aging, vol 19.* Springer, Cham. Retrieved from https://link.springer.com/chapter/10.1007/978-3-319-73820-8_11#citeas

19. Markov, C. Youngmin, Yoon. (2020). Diversity and age stereotypes in portrayals of older adults in popular American primetime television series. *Ageing and Society*, Cambridge University Press. Retrieved from https://www.cambridge.org/core/journals/ageing-and-society/article/abs/diversity-and-age-stereotypes-in-portrayals-of-older-adults-in-popular-american-primetime-television-series/46F3951791C966A8231E9C605FB48299

20. O'Grady, Natalie. "Target Audiences: What It Is and How to Find Yours." Web log. *Sprout Blog/Social Media Marketing* (blog). Sprout Blog, March 27, 2024. https://sproutsocial.com/insights/target-audience

21. Perkins, Lawrence. "Pharmaceutical Companies Must Make Decisions Based on Profit." *Western Journal of Medicine* 175, no. 6 (2001): 422–23. https://doi.org/https://pmc.ncbi.nlm.nih.gov/articles/PMC1275981

22. Sprout. "Social Listening: Your Launchpad to Success on Social Media." Web log. *Social Media Listening* (blog). Sprout Blog, July 25, 2024.https://sproutsocial.com/insights/social-media-listening

23. Stettner, Morey. "Movies That Portray Older People Real;Isticallyare Rare. Here Are a Few That Rise above Ageism and Stereotypes." *Retirement Weekly*, January 26, 2024. e-above-ageism-and-stereotypes-e93667e0

24. Taylor, C. (2022). Ageism in Advertising: Common Stereotypes and How to Avoid Them. *Forbes*. Retrieved from https://www.forbes.com/sites/charlesrtaylor/2022/03/11/ageism-in-advertising-common-stereotypes-and-how-to-avoid-them

CHAPTER 5: THE ANTI-AGING SCAM

1. Applewhite, A. (2000). *This Chair Rocks: A Manifesto Against Ageism*. New York: Celadon Books.

2. Baumann, Leslie. "Inside Cosmeceutical Market Claims." *Practical Dermatology*, May 5, 2012. https://practicaldermatology.com/topics/general-topics/inside-cosmeceutical-marketing-claims/21642/#:~:text=Often%20if%20a%20formulation%20is,study%20and%2For%20analysis%20of%20results

3. "Beauty and Fashion--Victorian Historian." *Victorian Historian*, February 2, 2023.https://thevictorianhistorian.com/beauty-fashion.

4. Brodmerkel, Sven, and Richie Barker. "Hitting the 'Glass Wall': Investigating Everyday Ageism in the Advertising Industry." *Sociological Review*, March 8, 2019.https://journals.sagepub.com/doi/abs/10.1177/0038026119837147

5. Carlton, Genevieve. "Queen Elizabeth I Was Probably Killed By the Makeup Required for Her Signature Look." *Ranker*, December 18, 2020.https://www.ranker.com/list/queen-elizabeth-i-makeup-effects/genevieve-carlton

6. "Cosmetics Marketing Strategies for 2025." *Hangar12*, 2025. https://www.hangar-12.com/blog/cosmetics-marketing-strategies-for-2025

7. Gendron, T. (2022). *Ageism Unmasked: Exploring Age Bias And How to End It*. New Hampshire: Steerforth Press L.L.C.

8. Haboush, A., Warren, C.S., Benuto, L. (2015, December 15). Beauty, Ethnicity, and Age: Does Internalization of Mainstream Media Ideals Influence Attitudes Towards Older Adults? *Research Gate.* Retrieved from https://www.researchgate.net/publication/257663656_Beauty_Ethnicity_and_Age_Does_Internalization_of_Mainstream_Media_Ideals_Influence_Attitudes_Towards_Older_Adults

9. James, Stuzin, and Rod J Rohrich. "Plastic and Reconstructive Surgery and Evolution of Cosmetic Surgery Education." *Plastic and Reconstructive Surgery,* March 2021. https://journals.lww.com/plasreconsurg/fulltext/2021/03000/plastic_and_reconstructive_surgery_and_the.49.aspx

10. Levy, B. (2022). *Breaking the Code: How Your Beliefs About Aging Determine How Long & Well You Live.* New York: Harper Collins.

11. "Men's Late Victorian Clothing (1870s-1890s)." *Historical Emporium,* March 4, 2023. https://www.historicalemporium.com/mens-late-victorian-clothing.php?srsltid=AfmBOorjfSCAiMc0ScpuxZzQ2csRfzXCnGVSybwNW4L3zvWMX2bWxoK8#:~:text=Victorian%20Ties%20%20,a%20bit%20of%20sartorial%20style

12. Morrison, Margaret. "Hypoallergenic Cosmetics." *Cosmetic and Labeling Claims,* February 25, 2025. https://www.fda.gov/cosmetics/cosmetics-labeling-claims/hypoallergenic-cosmetics#Historical_Background

13. Muse, T. (2024). *The Gibson Girl & Beyond: Ideals of Beauty in Edwardian Fashion.* Retrieved March 12, 2024, from https://www.historyoasis.com/post/edwardian-fashion

14. Reeves, Savannah R. "Beauty Is in the Eye of the Beholder: How Victorians Used Common Poisons to Become Drop Dead Gorgeous." *Historic Denver*, February 3, 2017. https://mollybrown.org/beauty-is-in-the-eye-of-the-beholder-how-victorians-used-common-poisons-to-become-drop-dead-gorgeous/#:~:text=multitude%20of%20side%20effects%20from,to%20cover%20up%20ts%20effects

15. Royal Museums Greenwich (n.d.). *Elizabeth the First's Fashion and Beauty: How did Elizabeth's tastes in clothing evolve during her reign?* https://www.rmg.co.uk/stories/royal-history/elizabeth-i-fashion-beauty

16. Sandhya, Pruthi, and Nicolas D Allen. "Tween and Teen Health." *Healthy Lifestyle*, January 18, 2024. https://www.mayoclinic.org/healthy-lifestyle/tween-and-teen-health/indepth/teens-and-social-media-use/art-20474437?utm_source=chatgpt.com

17. Schofield, Kinsey. "The Toxic Beauty Regime of the Virgin Queen--Queen Elizabeth's Makeup Routine." *To Di For Daily*, September 9, 2021. https://todifordaily.com/2021/09/the-toxic-beauty-regime-of-the-virgin-queen-queen-elizabeths-makeup-routine/#:~:text=She%20is%20sadly%20remembered%20as,years%20after%20Queen20Elizabeth%20died

18. Selby, Jenn. "Beauty Secrets from the Golden Age of Hollywood." *Glamour Newsletter*, May 23, 2016. https://www.glamourmagazine.co.uk/gallery/vintage-beauty-secrets-marilyn-monroe-grace-kelly-audrey-hepburn

19. Smithsonian. (n.d.). *Cosmetics and Personal Care Products in the Medicine & Science Collection.* Retrieved March 11, 2024, from https://www.si.edu/spotlight/health-hygiene-and-beauty/make-up

20. The Dose. (n.d.). The History of Skincare: From the Ancients to Personalism. *The Dose*. Retrieved from https://www.skinandme. com/the-dose/the-history-of-skincare

21. Wakeman, A. (2024, Jan./Feb). Rethinking Jessica DeFino. *Country & Town House*. Retrieved July 24, 2024, from https:// www.countryandtownhouse.com/style/health-and-beauty/ jessica-defino-interview

22. "Was Queen Elizabeth I Poisoned?" *Wonderopolis*, February 4, 2022. https://wonderopolis.org/wonder/Was-Queen-Elizabeth-I-Poisoned#:~:text=Lead%20may%20not%20 have%20been,also%20contributed%20to%20her%20illness

23. Whitfords (n.d.). *Men's Skincare: From Ancient History to Modern Trends*. Retrieved July 24, 2024, from https://www. whitfords.co.uk/mens-skincare-from-ancient-history-to-modern-trend

CHAPTER 6: MINDFULNESS

1. Attia, P. (2023). Outlive: Work in Progress: The High Price of Ignoring Emotional Health. In *Outlive: The Science & Art of Longevity* (pp. 377-408). New York: Penguin Random House.

2. Brown, J, & Wong, J. (2017). Greater Good Magazine: Science-Based Insights for A Meaningful Life. *How Gratitude Changes You and Your Brain*. Retrieved February 19, 2024, from https:// greatergood.berkeley.edu/article/item/how_gratitude_changes_ you_and_your_brain

3. Collard, P. (n.d.). *The Little Book of Mind Fullness: 10 Minutes a Day to Less Stress, More Peace*. GAIA Press.

4. Dharma, Dough. "Mindfulness of Breathing Practice: Body and Feelings." *Dough Darma's Institute*. Lecture presented at the Mindfulness, April 29, 2025. https://www.youtube.com/watch?v=fpcP0Oim4jE

5. Flyn, James. "Buddha and Mind." Humanities, September 2021. https://www.neh.gov/article/buddha-and-mind?utm_source=chatgpt.com

6. Hanson, R. Greater Good Magazine: Science-Based Insights for A Meaningful Life. *How to Grow the Good in Your Brain*. Retrieved February 19, 2024, from https://greatergood.berkeley.edu/article/item/how_to_grow_the_good_in_your_brain

7. Kennedy, Quinn. "Why Learning Mindfulness Will Be Easier yet Also Challenging." Aging and Mindfulness, December 15, 2022. https://www.psychologytoday.com/us/blog/aging-and-mindfulness/202212/aging-and-mindfulness

8. Kristina, J. (2017). What is Mindfulness? And How Does it Help Decrease Anxiety. [Video]. YouTube. Retrieved from https://www.youtube.com/watch?v=4zDSF9pTVOc

9. LaPlante, Justin. "History of Mindfulness." Human Resources and Organizational Excellence. Accessed April 29, 2025. https://www.clarku.edu/humanresources/2021/11/22/history-of-mindfulness/?utm_source=chatgpt.com

10. McLeod, Julianna. Stress Relief: Mindfulness Techniques for Seniors and Caregivers, February 23, 2024. https://allseniorscare.com/stress-relief-mindfulness-techniques-for-seniors-and-caregivers.

11. Rezac, M. (2021). *Mindfulness Activities for Adults: 50 Simple Exercises to Relax, Stay Present, and Find Peace*. California: Rockbridge Press.

12. Selva, Joaquin. "The History and Origins of Mindfulness-Positive Psychology.Com." Mindfulness, March 13, 2017. https://positivepsychology.com/history-of-mindfulness/?utm_source=chatgpt.com

13. Suttie, J. (2023, December 4). Greater Good Magazine: Science-Based Insights for A Meaningful Life. *Five Ways Mindfulness Helps You Age Better*. Retrieved February 28, 2024, from https://greatergood.berkeley.edu/article/item/five_ways_mindfulness_helps_you_age_better

14. UC San Diego: Extended Studies. (n.d.). *Unlocking Healthy Aging: Learning, Community, and Mindfulness*. Retrieved April 9, 2024, from https://extendedstudies.ucsd.edu/olli/about-us/osher-news/unlocking-healthy-aging-learning-community-and-mindfulness

15. Vago, David R, and Fadel Zeidan. "The Brain on Silent: Mind Wandering, Mindful Awareness, and States of Mental Tranquility." *The New York Academy of Sciences* July 11, 2016. https://nyaspubs.onlinelibrary.wiley.com/doi/full/10.1111/nyas.13171

16. Wang, Yun-Hang, Yun-Lin Wang, Dara Kiu Leung, Zuna Loong Ng, and Oscar Chan. "Effectiveness of an Age-Modified Mindfulness-Based Cognitive Therapy (MBCT) in Improving Mental Health in Older People with Depressive Symptoms: A Non-Randomized Controlled Trial." *Pub Med*, February 26, 2025. https://pubmed.ncbi.nlm.nih.gov/40011881

17. Wong, S. H. (2024). *Mindfulness for Brain Health*. EBH Press.

18. Zinn, J.K. (2013). What is Mindfulness? (Video). YouTube. https://www.youtube.com/watch?v=HmEo6RI4Wvs&list=PLMSFhxxMz78VZaxVQkwUR6H1ur5iUs9oI

CHAPTER 7: CONTINUOUS LEARNING

1. Harrogate. (n.d.). The Importance of Lifelong Learning for Seniors. *Harrogate.* Retrieved from https://www.harrogatelifecare.org/news/the-importance-of-lifelong-learning-for-seniors

2. Institute on Aging. (n.d.). Still You, Always You: Aging Doesn't Mean You Stop Growing. *Institute on Aging.* Retrieved from https://www.ioaging.org/aging/aging-doesnt-mean-you-stop-growing

3. Kakulla, B. (2022). Lifelong Learning Attracts Older Adults for Personal Growth and Cognitive Health. *AARP.* Retrieved from https://www.aarp.org/research/topics/life/info-2022/lifelong-learning-older-adults.html

4. Lifelong Learning. (2017, December 22). Learning How to Learn with Barbara Oakley. *Lifelong Learning.* Retrieved from https://www.ie.edu/lifelong-learning/blog/notes-from-ie-lifelong-learning/learning-learn-barbara-oakley

5. Narushima M, Liu j, Diestelkamp N. Lifelong learning in active ageing discourse: its conserving effect on wellbeing, health and vulnerability. *Ageing and Society.* 2018;38(4):651-675. doi:10.1017/S0144686X16001136

6. Nelson, K. (2023). The Cognitive Benefits of Lifelong Learning for Older Adults. Retrieved on March 11, 12024 from https://www.knutenelson.org/news-stories/lifelong-learning-benefits

7. Purdue-Spears, C. (2022). *Four Benefits of Lifelong Learning for Older Adults.* Blog. Retrieved March 11, 2024, from https://familymattershc.com/benefits-of-lifelong-learning-for-seniors

8. Salvesen, M. (2023). Boosting Senior Brain Health Through the Power of Cognitive Activities & Games. UMH. Retrieved on March 13, 2024, from https://www.umh.org/assisted-independent-living-blog/boosting-senior-brain-health#:~:text=Enhancing%20Memory%20%26%20Learning%3A%20Memory%2D,combat%20age%2Drelated%20memory%20decline

9. Seasons Retirement Communities (n.d.). Ten Benefits of Lifelong Learning for Older Adults. Retrieved March 11, 2024, from https://seasonsretirement.com/benefits-of-lifelong-learning

10. The Life Institute. (2021, July 15). Lifelong Learning for Healthy Aging. *The Life Institute.* Retrieved from https://thelifeinstitute.ca/page/Lifelong-Learning-for-Healthy-Aging

CHAPTER 8: FINDING YOUR PASSION IN LIFE

1. Applewhite, Ashton. *This Chair Rocks: A Manifesto Against Ageism.* New York: Celadon Books, 2020.

2. Athuly (2018). Five Reasons to Pursue Your Passion as yokj u www.athulyaliving.com/blogs/5-reasons-pursue-passion-age.php

3. Coxwell, Kathleen. "Prepare for Life After Retirement: 6 Ways to Find Meaning and Purpose for This Stage of Life." *Boldin,* 2024. https://www.boldin.com/retirement/prepare-life-retirement-ways-find-meaning-purpose-stage-life

4. Davidson, Nicola. "Finding a Purpose in Life Can Empower Older Adults to Thrive." *Hebrew Senior Life*, September 23, 2024. https://www.hebrewseniorlife.org/blog/finding-purpose-life-can-empower-older-adults-thrive

5. DeCost, Sally. "Five Reasons to Follow Your Passions." *Elementary Matters*. Accessed May 5, 2025. https://www.elementarymatters.com/2024/10/follow-your-passions.html

6. D'Arrigo, Terri. "Ageism Takes Toll on Physical, Mental Health." *Psychiatric News*, August 22, 2022. https://psychiatryonline.org/doi/full/10.1176/appi.pn.2022.09.9.5

7. *Five Ways to Find Your Passions in Retirement*. United States: Second Wind Movement. Accessed May 31, 2025. https://www.youtube.com/watch?v=VUPqijqQBfQ

8. Fritz. (2020, November 11). *How to Find Your Passion in Retirement (A Reader's Story)*. [On forum post]. Retrieved on August 31, 2024, from https://www.theretirementmanifesto.com/how-to-find-your-passion-in-retirement-a-readers-story

9. Gigante, S. (2024, March 05). *10 Ways to Find Meaning and Purpose in Retirement*. [Online forum post. Mass Mutual. Retrieved August 31, 2024, from https://blog.massmutual.com/retiring-investing/purpose-retirement

10. Hively, H. "How to Rediscover Your Passions and Hobbies in Retirement." *Hively Collection*, April 3, 2025. https://www.joinhively.com/post/how-to-rediscover-your-passions-and-hobbies-in-retirement

11. Irving, Justine. "Just Get Up and Get On: Purpose in Later Life." Activities, *Adaptation & Aging*, February 6, 2024. https://www. tandfonline.com/doi/epdf/10.1080/01924788.2024.2317013? needAccess=true

12. Knee, Mallory. "Reclaiming Passions in Later Life: Rediscovering Joy and Purpose as an Older Adult." *LTC News*, December 4, 2024. https://www.ltcnews.com/articles/reclaiming-passions-later-life-rediscovering-joy-purpose-older-adult

13. Lavoy, G. (2022). The Nurture of Passion as You Age: The soul and spirit don't retire even if your career does. *Psychology Today.* https://www.psychologytoday.com/us/blog/passion/202209/ the-nurture-passion-you-age

14. Lennon, Annie. "Passion, Exercise, and Meaningful Relationships Are a Boon to Brain Health." New Normal Health, September 28, 2022. https://www.medicalnewstoday. com/articles/passion-exercise-and-relationships-protect-against-cognitive-decline

15. Levy, Becca. *Breaking The Age Code: How Your Beliefs About Aging Determine How Long & Well You Live.* New York: William Morrow, 2023.

16. Levy, B. (2022). Later-Life Mental Health Growth. *Breaking the Age Code* (pp. 73-90). New York: Harper Collins

17. Meyer, C. (n.d.). 5 Steps to Finding Your Passions After Retirement. *Second Wind Movement.* Retrieved from https:// secondwindmovement.com/finding-passions

18. "Passion, Exercise, and Meaningful Relationships Are Boon to Brain Health." *New Normal Health*, September 28,

2022. https://www.medicalnewstoday.com/articles
/passion-exercise-and-relationships-protect-against-cognitive-
decline

19. Reid, T.R. (2024, April/May). The Deep Need to Live a Life of
Purpose. *AARP.*

20. Rodriguez, D. (2021, October 6). 5 Tips for Older Adults to
Rediscover Your Passions. *Tapestry Senior Living.* Retrieved from
https://www.tapestrysenior.com/2021/10/06/5-tips-for-older-
adults-to-rediscover-your-passions

21. *Tapestry Senior Living* (n.d.). Five Tips for Older Adults to
Rediscover Your Passions. Retrieved on April 16, 2024.

22. Athulya (2018). Five Reasons to Pursue Your Passion as You
Age. 7www.athulyaliving.com/blogs/5-reasons-pursue-passion-
age.php

23. Fritz. (2020, November 11). *How to Find Your Passion
in Retirement (A Reader's Story).* [On forum post]. Retrieved
on August 31, 2024, from https://www.theretirement
manifesto.com/how-to-find-your-passion-in-retirement-a-
readers-stor

24. Gigante, S. (2024, March 05). *10 Ways to Find Meaning and
Purpose in Retirement.* [Online forum post. Mass Mutual.
Retrieved August 31, 2024, from https://blog.massmutual.com/
retiring-investing/purpose-retirement

25. Lavoy, G. (2022). The Nurture of Passion as You Age: The soul
and spirit don't retire even if your career does. *Psychology Today.*
https://www.psychologytoday.com/us/blog/passion/202209/
the-nurture-passion-you-age

26. Levy, B. (2022). Later-Life Mental Health Growth. *Breaking the Age Code* (pp. 73-90). New York: Harper Collins

27. Meyer, C. (n.d.). 5 Steps to Finding Your Passions After Retirement. *Second Wind Movement*. Retrieved from https://secondwindmovement.com/finding-passions

28. Reid, T.R. (2024, April/May). The Deep Need to Live a Life of Purpose. *AARP*.

29. Rodriguez, D. (2021, October 6). 5 Tips for Older Adults to Rediscover Your Passions. *Tapestry Senior Living*. Retrieved from https://www.tapestrysenior.com/2021/10/06/5-tips-for-older-adults-to-rediscover-your-passions

30. *Tapestry Senior Living* (n.d.). Five Tips for Older Adults to Rediscover Your Passions. Retrieved on April 16, 2024

CHAPTER 9: TECHNOLOGY TO THE RESCUE?

1. Andersen, G.O. (2016). Americans' Future Technology Needs and Wants. *AARP*. https://www.aarp.org/pri/topics/technology/internet-media-devices/americans-future-tech-needs-wants

2. Andersen, G.O. & Thayer, C. (2018). Loneliness and Social Connections: A National Survey of Adults 45 and Older. *AARP*. https://www.aarp.org/research/topics/life/info-2018/loneliness-social-connections.html

3. Andersen, T & Nerlyn, D. (2023). Smart Aging: Emerging Technology to Improve the Lives of Older Adults. YouTube. https://www.youtube.com/watch?v=2MLTn87qdsE

4. Berlyn, D. (2023, February 10). *Tech Innovations That Are Improving the Way We Age*. Personal Care. https://www.ncoa.org/article/tech-innovations-that-are-improving-the-way-we-age/

5. Cutler, S. J. (2005). Ageism and Technology. *Generations: Journal of the American Society on Aging,* 29(3), 67–72. https://www.jstor.org/stable/26555416

6. Czaja, S. J., & Barr, R. A. (1989). Technology and the Everyday Life of Older Adults. *The Annals of the American Academy of Political and Social Sciences.* https://www.jstor.org/stable/1047222?searchText=&searchUri=&ab_segments=&searchKey=&refreqid=fastly-default%3A838f7ea82b6f73b9588a98fc570f3b38&seq=2

7. Freeman, S., Marston, H. R., Olynick, J., Kulczycki, C., Genoe, R., & Xiong, B. (2020). "Intergenerational Effects on the Impacts of Technology Use in Later Life: Insights from an International, Multi-Site Study." *International Journal of Environmental Research and Public Health.* https://doi.org/10.3390/ijerph17165711

8. Gendron, T. (2022). *Ageism unmasked: Exploring age bias and how to end it*. Steerforth Press.

9. Kakulla, B. (2023). Older Adults Embrace Tech but Are Skeptical of AI. *AARP.* https://www.aarp.org/pri/topics/technology/internet-media-devices/2024-technology-trends-older-adults.html

10. Leung, C., Wong, K. C., Li, W. W. Y., Cao, Y., & Shum, D. H. K. (2022, June 8). The Application of Technology to Improve Cognition in Older Adults: A Review and Suggestions for Future Directions. *PsyCh Journal.* Wiley Online Library. https://onlinelibrary.wiley.com/doi/10.1002/pchj.565

11. Levy, B. (2023). *Breaking the age code: How your beliefs about aging determine how long & well you live.* William Morrow.

12. Nash, S. (2019, April 13). *Older Adults and Technology: Moving Beyond the Stereotypes.* Standford Center for Longevity. https://longevity.stanford.edu/older-adults-and-technology-moving-beyond-the-stereotypes

13. Pelizaus-Hoffmeister. (2016). Motives of the Elderly for the Use of Technology in their Daily Lives. *Ageing and Technology: Perspectives from the Social Sciences.* https://www.jstor.org/stable/j.ctv1xxrwd.4?searchText=&searchUri=&ab_segments=&searchKey=&refreqid=fastly-default%3A464e195fb84cfda94ae61dc689fa70df&seq=19

14. Salter, J. (2023, November 6). *6 Benefits of Technology for Seniors.* Caring Senior Services. https://caringseniorservice.com

15. Seegert, L. (2023). The Best Technology to Prevent Falls, Monitor Safety, and Help Older Adults Age in Place Longer. Retrieved on April 20, 2024, from https://fortune.com/well/2023/02/03/technology-can-help-older-adults-age-in-place-longer/https://caringseniorservice.com

16. Sen, K., Prybutok, G., & Prybutok, V. (2022, March 1). *The Use of Digital Technology for Social Wellbeing Reduces Social Isolation in Older Adults: A Systematic Review. Science Direct.* https://www.sciencedirect.com/science/article/pii/S23528273321002950?via%3Dihub

17. Stokes, K. (2025, June 13). *Keep these simple steps in mind--and share them with family and friends-to fight back against today's sophisticated fraud criminals.* AARP's New Message to Stay Safe

from Scams: Pause. Reflect. Protect. https://www.aarp.org/
money/scams-fraud/pause-reflect-protect

18. Vaughn, D. & Stover, L (2021). Older Adults and Technology.
YouTube. https://www.youtube.com/watch?v=18hP-LZqllY

CHAPTER 10: EXERCISE

1. Attia, P. Outlive: Work in Progress: The High Price of Ignoring
Emotional Health. In *Outlive: The Science & Art of Longevity*,
377-408. New York: Penguin Random House, 2023.

2. Cappello, Tiffani. "How Mindset Shapes Health and Healing."
Transformational Hypnosis and Coaching, January 21, 2025. https://
tiffanicappello.com/how-mindset-shapes-health-and-healing

3. Crouch, Michelle. "The Number 1 Exercise to Do as You Get
Older." *Health*, 2022. https://www.aarp.org/health/healthy-
living/squats-best-exercise-for-strength/#:~:text=%E2%80%9
CSquats%20are%20one%20of%20the,our%20knees%20and%20
our%20hips.%E2%80%9D.

4. Griffin, M. R. "Myths About Exercising and Older Adult."
WebMD. Last modified February 23, 2021. Accessed May 1,
2024. *(Note: While the source implies WebMD, the precise URL
was not provided in the original excerpt for Griffin. The URL
from Ch 10 List of notes.pdf is used here: https://www.webmd.
com/healthy-aging/features/exercise-older-adults.)*

5. Harms, M. "Personal Trainer Advises Us to Get Stronger for
Better Balance." *3rd Act: Aging with Confidence*, spring 2024, 51.

6. Harms, M. "The Quest for Strength." *3rd Act: Aging with
Confidence*, winter 2023/2024, 30-31.

7. Heart To Heart Home Care. "Fall Prevention for Seniors:
    The Ultimate Guide." Last modified February 26, 2025. https://
    h2hhc.com/blog/fall-prevention-for-seniors-the-ultimate-guide

8. Hickerson, Ali. "How Physical Inactivity Impacts You as You
    Age." *Newsroom*, April 1, 2024. https://www.northwell.edu/
    news/the-latest/physical-inactivity-impacts-you-as-you-age

9. Hou, Bin, Yuxin Wu, and Yuqi Huang. "Physical exercise and
    mental health among older adults: the mediating role of social
    competence." *Frontiers in Public Health* 12 (June 19, 2024):
    1385166. https://doi.org/10.3389/fpubh.2024.1385166

10. Langhammer, B., A. Bergland, and E. Rydwik. "The Importance
    of Physical Activity Exercising Among Older People."
    BioMed Research International 1 (2018). Accessed May
    1, 2024. *(Note: The original excerpt for Langhammer et al.
    did not provide the precise URL. The URL from Ch 10 List
    of notes.pdf is used here: https://onlinelibrary.wiley.com/
    doi/10.1155/2018/7856823)*

11. Levy, Becca R. *Breaking the Code: How Your Beliefs About Aging
    Determine How Long & Well Live.* New York: Harper Collins, 2022.

12. Levy, Becca R., Corey Pilver, Pil H Chung, and Martin D
    Slade. "Subliminal strengthening: improving older individuals'
    physical function over time with an implicit-age-stereotype
    intervention." *Psychological Science* 25, no. 12 (December 2014):
    2127–35. https://doi.org/10.1177/0956797614551970

13. Levy, Becca R., and Martin D. Slade. "Positive views of aging reduce
    risk of developing later-life obesity." *Preventive Medicine Reports* 13
    (2019): 196–198. https://doi.org/10.1016/j.pmedr.2018.12.012

14. National Council of Aging. "The Life Changing Benefits of Exercise After 60." National Council on Aging. Last modified August 30, 2021. Accessed May 2, 2024. https://www.ncoa.org/article/the-life-changing-benefits-of-exercise-after-60

15. National Institute on Aging. *Exercise & Physical Activity: Your Everyday Guide.* Washington, D.C.: U.S. Department of Health and Human Services, [n.d.]. Accessed May 10, 2024. https://go4life.nia.nih.gov

16. Seegert, L. "4 Ways Exercise Helps Fight Aging." Time. Accessed May 2, 2024. *(Note: The original excerpt for Seegert did not provide the precise URL. The URL from Ch 10 List of notes.pdf is used here: https://time.com/6053055/how-exercise-fights-aging)*

17. Seguin, Rebecca A., Jacqueline N. Epping, David M. Buchner, Rina Bloch, and Miriam E. Nelson. *Growing Stronger: Strength Training for Older Adults.* Atlanta: Centers for Disease Control and Prevention; Boston: Tufts University, 2002. Accessed May 10, 2024. www.nutrition.tufts.edu/growingstronger

18. U.S. Department of Health and Human Services. *Physical Activity Guidelines for Americans, 2nd edition.* Washington, D.C.: U.S. Department of Health and Human Services, 2018. https://odphp.health.gov/PAGuidelines

CHAPTER 11: NUTRITION

1. Alzra. "Foods for Healthy Brain and Enhanced Memory." Alzheimer's Research Association, June 14, 2024. https://www.alzra.org/blog/foods-for-healthy-brain-and-enhanced-memory

2.   Attia, P. (2023). Outlive: Work in Progress: The High Price of Ignoring Emotional Health. In *Outlive: The Science & Art of Longevity* (pp. 291-306, 311-316, 322--330). New York: Penguin Random House.

3.   Axe, J. (2020). How to read a nutrition label – Nutrition Labels 101 [Video]. YouTube. https://www.youtube.com/watch?v=cAzQbaH2h2U&t=18s

4.   Balduzzi, A. (2020). How to read nutrition information: Food labels explained [Video]. YouTube. https://www.youtube.com/watch?v=hbUxV19x3Bw

5.   Cleveland Clinic. (2023). Nutrition for older adults: why eating well matters as you age. *Cleveland Clinic.* Retrieved May 8, 2024, from https://health.clevelandclinic.org/how-to-age-better-by-eating-more-healthfully

6.   Co, J. (2021). How to read nutrition labels and the potential impact on your health. *Oak Street Health.* Retrieved on May 16, 2024, from https://www.oakstreethealth.com/how-to-read-nutrition-labels-and-potential-impacts-on-your-health-551148

7.   Department of Agriculture, US. "Eat Healthy on a Budget." USDA Food and Nutrition Service. Accessed March 3, 2022. https://myplate-prod.azureedge.us/sites/default/files/2024-06/TipSheet-23-Eat-Healthy-On-A-Budget.pdf

8.   De Silva, D. (2021). Nutrition as we age: Healthy eating with dietary guidelines. *Health.gov, OASH.* Retrieved on May 8, 2024, from https://health.gov/news/202107/nutrition-we-age-healthy-eating-dietary-guidelines

9. Harguth, Anne. "Eating Healthy on a Budget." Speaking of Health, April 26, 2022. https://www.mayoclinichealthsystem. org/hometown-health/speaking-of-health/eating-healthy-on-a-budget

10. "6 Tips for Healthy Eating on a Budget." *Idaho Foodbank*. Idaho Foodbank, February 8, 2017. https://idahofoodbank.org/news

11. Kadey, M. (2023). How to read the new nutrition labels and why it matters. *Silver Sneakers*. Retrieved on May 16, 2024, from https://www.silversneakers.com/blog/how-to-read-the-new-nutrition-labels-and-why-it-matters

12. Medline Plus (n.d.). Nutrition for Older Adults. *National Institute on Aging*. Retrieved on May 7,2024, from https:// medlineplus.gov/nutritionforolderadults.html

13. My Plate. (n.d.). Eating healthy has benefits that can help people ages 60 and up. *U.S. Department of Agriculture*. Retrieved on May 7, 2024, from https://www.myplate.gov/life-stages/older-adults

14. NIH. (n.d.). How to read food and beverage labels. *The National Institute of Aging*. Retrieved on May 7, 2024, from https://www. nia.nih.gov/health/healthy-eating-nutrition-and-diet/how-read-food-and-beverage-labels

15. Pankey, Madison, and Hannah Halusker. "Fueling the Aging Brain: How Nutrition Boosts Cognitive Health and Memory." Colorado State University, 2024. https://www.research. colostate.edu/healthyagingcenter/2024/11/05/fueling-the-aging-brain-how-nutrition-boosts-cognitive-health-and-memory

16. Selhub, Eva. "Nutrition: A Key Modulator of Cognitive Health."
Nutritional psychiatry: Your brain on food, September 18, 2022.
https://www.health.harvard.edu/blog/nutritional-psychiatry-
your-brain-on-food-201511168626

17. "Senior Citizen Nutrition Tips: How to Eat Healthy on a Budget."
Amy Group Insurance, 2024. https://www.amyins.com/article/
senior-citizen-nutrition-tips-how-to-eat-healthy-on-budget

18. West, H. (2019). 8 Ways the food companies hide sugar content
of food. *Healthline*. Retrieved on May 16, 2024, from https://
www.healthline.com/nutrition/8-ways-sugar-is-hidden

CHAPTER 12: AGING IN PLACE OR RETIREMENT COMMUNITIES

1. Aronson, Louise. "How Medicine Fails Old People." Association
of American Medical Colleges, October 1, 2024. https://www.
aamc.org/news/how-medicine-fails-older-people

2. Bukhari, Sam. "Pros & Cons of Aging in Place: A Complete
List." Evolution Walker, May 10, 2024. https://evolutionwalker.
com/pros-cons-of-aging-in-place-a-complete-list

3. Carlozo, Lou. "Should You Avoid Living in a 55-plus
Community? Here Are 5 Big Problems with Adult Retirement
Communities in America." AOL, April 6, 2024. https://www.
aol.com/finance/a

4. Clow, Chris. "Older Americans Are 'Splurging' on Home
Modifications to Support Aging in Place." *Housing Wire*,
May 22, 2024. https://www.housingwire.com/articles/older-
americans-are-splurging-on-home-modifications-to-support-
aging-in-place

5. Conde, Arturo. "The Cost of Living in a Retirement Community in Every State." Retirement Planning, March 4, 2024. https://smartasset.com/retirement/cost-of-retirement-communities

6. Fausett, Cara Bailey, Andrew J Kelly, Wendy A Rogers, and Arthur D Fisk. "Challenges to Aging in Place: Understanding Home Maintenance Difficulties." PMC PubMed Central, April 1, 2012. https://pmc.ncbi.nlm.nih.gov/articles/PMC3209521

7. *Freedom, Mortgage.* "What Are the Pros and Cons of 55+ Communities?" Freedom Mortgage, October 1, 2024. https://www.freedommortgage.com/learning-center/articles/pros-cons-55-communities

8. Funds, Hartford. "How to Decide: Aging in Place vs. Assisted Living." https://www.hartfordfunds.com/insights/investor-insight/navigating-longevity/retirement/how-to-decide.html, November 21, 2022. https://www.hartfordfund

9. Gaines, Shaneece. "Can You Afford to Age in Place?" Housing & Equity Resources, August 4, 2023. https://www.ncoa.org/article/can-you-afford-to-age-in-place

10. Gleckman, Howard. "A Valuable New Framework For Improving The Care Of Frail Older Adults." Howard Gleckman, September 7, 2022. https://howardgleckman.com/2022/09/07/a-valuable-new-framework-for-improving-the-care-of-frail-older-adults

11. Hendricks, Mark. "The Cost of Living in a Retirement Community in Every State." Retirement Planning, March 4, 2024. https://smartasset.com/retirement/cost-of-retirement-communities

12. L & H Lutheran Home, Harwood. "Assisted Living Homes vs. Aging in Place: Making an Informed Decision." L & H, January 1, 2024. https://www.thelutheranhome.org/assisted-living-homes-vs-aging-in-place

13. Lim, Weng Marc, and Carmen Bowan. "Aging in a Place of Choice." Activities, Adaptation & Aging, July 1, 2022. https://doi.org/10.1080/01924788.2022.2097806

14. Marshall, Katherine, and Deborah Hale. "Aging in Place." Pub Med, May 1, 2020. https://pubmed.ncbi.nlm.nih.gov/32358444

15. Mroz, Ralph. "The Disadvantages Of Aging In Place." More from Forbes, September 25, 2020. https://www.forbes.com/sites/nextavenue/2020/09/25/the-disadvantages-of-aging-in-place

16. Neely, Dawn. "Aging in Place: YouTube." April 1, 2023.

17. Owusa, Brenda, Balkys Bevins, Remy Marseille, and Diana Lyn Baptiste. "Aging in Place: Programs, Challenges and Opportunities for Promoting Healthy Aging for Older Adults." School of Nursing, 2023. https://pure.johnshopkins.edu/en/publications/aging-in-place-programs-challenges-and-opportunities-for-promotion

18. Perry, Mark. "Aging in Place Benefits: A Comprehensive Guide to Pros, Cons, and Real-Life Examples." Age Well Senior Fitness LLC, October 30, 2023. https://agewellseniorfitness.com/aging-in-place-benefits-a-comprehensive-guide-to-pros-cons-and-real-life-examples-2

19. Right, At Home. "What Is Aging in Place? All You Need to Know." Home/Senior Care, 2024. https://www.rightathome.net/central-texas/blog/what-is-aging-in-place-all-you-need-to-know

20. Senior, Life Insights. "Senior Living Community Vs. Aging in Place: What's Best For You?" Maplewood, 2024. https://www.maplewoodseniorliving.com/blog/senior-living-community-vs-aging-in-place-whats-best-for-you

21. Some Nursing Homes vs Aging in Place – What's Safer, Cheaper, and Happier? Nursing Homes vs Aging in Place – What's Safer, Cheaper, and Happier? Senior Life Insights, 2025. https://www.youtube.com/watch?v=Q8jyysQGBUQ&t=2s

22. Span, Paula. "Why Cameras Are Popping Up in Eldercare Facilities." The New Old Age, April 7, 2025. https://www.nytimes.com/2025/04/07/health/cameras-assisted-living.html

23. The "Cedars." "Aging in Place vs Long Term Care Centers." Enhancing Lives Through All Stages of Living, 2024. https://thecedars.org/2024/04/23/aging-in-place-vs-long-term-care-centers

24. Van Leeuwen, Karen M, Miriam S Van Loon, Fenna A Van Nes, Judith E Bosmans, Henrica CW deVet, Johannes CF Ket, Guy AM Widderershoven, and Raymond WJG Ostelo. "What Does Quality of Life Mean to Older Adults? A Thematic Synthesis." Pub Med, March 8, 2019. https://pubmed.ncbi.nlm.nih.gov/30849098

25. Vitalia. " Aging in Place: What Are the Options?" Vitalia, 2024. https://vitaliarockside.com/blog/aging-in-place-what-are-the-options

CHAPTER 13: THE POWER OF ART AND MUSIC

1. Alain, C., Moussard, A., Singer, J., Lee, Y., Bidelman, G. M., & Moreno, S. (2019). Music and Visual Art Training Modulate Brain Activity in Older Adults. *Frontiers in Neuroscience, 13*, 434295. Retrieved from https://doi.org/10.3389/fnins.2019.00182

2. All About. 2025. "Can Music and Art Therapy Support Cognitive Longevity?" *All About Health Medical*. All About Health Medical. https://allabouthealthmedical.com/can-music-and-art-therapy-support-cognitive-longevity

3. Avanti (2023, February 7th). The Importance of Music and Art Therapy for Seniors. *Avanti Senior Living—Vision Park*. Retrieved from https://visionpark.avanti-sl.com/the-importance-of-music-and-art-therapy-for-seniors

4. Bagan, B. (n.d.). Aging: What's Art Got to do with It. *Ottawa University in Phoenix, AZ.*   Retrieved from https://transitionslifecare.org/wp-content/uploads/2016/06/Vol-7-16-Aging-Whats-Art-Got-to-Do-With-It.pdf

5. Colapinto, J. (2023, November 22). The Extradentary World of Music and the Mind. *AARP*. Retrieved from https://www.aarp.org/health/brain-health/info-2023/how-music-affects-the-brain.html

6. Fioranelli, Massimo, Maria Grazia Roccia, Maria Luisa Garo. 2023. "The Role of Arts Engagement in Reducing Cognitive Decline and Improving Quality of Life in Healthy Older People: A Systematic Review." *Frontiers in Psychology*. PubMed Central. August 21. https://www.ncbi.nlm.nih.gov/pmc/articles/PMC10475943

7. Garo, Maria Luisa, Massimo Fioranelli, Naria Grazia Roccia. 2023. "The Role of Arts Engagement in Reducing Cognitive Decline and Improving Quality of Life in Healthy Older People: A Systematic Review." *Frontiers*. https://www.frontiersin.org/journals/psychology/articles/10.3389/fpsyg.2023.1232357/full

8. Juniper. 2025. "The Impact of Art On Brain Health." *Juniper Senior Living.* Juniper Senior Living. March 25. https://junipercommunities.com/arts-for-seniors-importance-of-healthy-creative-aging/#h-the-impact-of-art-on-brain-health

9. Maddox, Fermina. (2023). The Importance of Art and Music for Seniors. *Liberty Resources: Home Choices.* Retrieved from https://www.homechoices.org/the-importance-of-art-and-music-for-seniors

10. McQuade, L, and R O'Sullivan. 2021. "Arts and Creativity in Later Life: Implications for Health and Wellbeing in Older Adults: Executive Summary." *Institute of Public Health* Executive Summary (ISBN: 978-1-913829-12-4): One-Fifteen. doi:10.14655/11971-1084888

11. Mintzer, J., (n.d.). Music and Brain Health. *AARP.* Retrieved from https://www.aarp.org/health/brain-health/global-council-on-brain-health/music

12. MTCCA, Antoine Crystal. 2016."Perceptions of Music Therapy Among Health Care Clinicians: Implications of Effective Interdisciplinary Collaboration.

13. Senior Friendship Centers. (n.d.). Creative Arts and Aging: The Benefits of Art Therapy. *Alumni Association.* Retrieved from https://friendshipcenters.org/creative-arts-and-aging-the-benefits-of-art-therapy

14. Stephenson, R. (n.d.). How Creative Expression Can Benefit Older Adults. *Lesley University.* Retrieved from https://lesley.edu/article/how-creative-expression-can-benefit-older-adults

15. UCLA Health. 2025. "How Music Therapy Helps Older Adults." *UCLA Health*. UCLA Health. April 1. https://www.uclahealth.org/news/how-music-therapy-helps-older-adults

CHAPTER 14: ADAPTATION IS OUR SILVER LINING

1. Aston Gardens. (n.d.). Adaptability: *A Skill Every Senior Needs*. Retrieved from https://www.astongardens.com/senior-living-blog/adaptability-a-skill-every-senior-needs

2. Attia, P. (2023). Outlive: The Science & Art of Longevity. *Work in Progress: The High Price of Ignoring Emotional Health* (pp. 377-408). New York: Harmony House.

3. Bakken, S. (2015, August 17). 7 Age-related Changes and How to Adapt. *Walker Methodist*. Retrieved from https://www.walkermethodist.org/blog/7-age-related-changes-how-to-adapt

4. Cassidy. K. A. "62 Leadership Resilience Quotes: How Great Leaders Overcome Challenges." Kerry Anne Cassidy, August 6, 2025. https://kerryannecassidy.com/resilience/leadership-resilience-quotes

5. Comforting Home Care. (2023, July 18). 10 Tips to Help Seniors Adjust to Change. *Comforting Home Care*. Retrieved from https://www.comfortinghome.com/posts/10-tips-to-help-seniors-adjust-to-change

6. Donohue, Melanie. Donohue, Melanie. "Causes and Effects of Financial Anxiety on Seniors." Blue Moon Senior Counseling, June 23, 2023. https://bluemoonseniorcounseling.com/causes-and-effects-of-financial-anxiety-on-seniors

7. Friedan, Betty. Betty Friedan Quotes, February 4, 2006. https://www.brainyquote.com/quotes/betty_friedan_383994

8. Heiser, D. Heiser, Deborah. "5 Common Fears About Growing Older." Psychology Today, 2023. https://www.psychologytoday.com/us/blog/the-right-side-of-40/202307/five-common-fears-about-growing-older

9. Hochman, D. (2024, June/July). One Woman's Search for Happiness. *AARP Magazine*. 60-65.

10. Keller, S. (2022, October 19th). Tips to Help Seniors Accept and Adapt to Changes. *Alternatives for Seniors*. Retrieved from https://www.alternativesforseniors.com/senior-resources/articles/adapt-to-change

11. Leardi, J. (n.d.). Age and the Potential to Change. *Changing Aging with Dr. Bill Thomas*. Retrieved from https://changingaging.org/blog/age-and-the-potential-to-change

12. Leardi, J. (n.d.). The Six Assets of Aging. *Changing Aging with Dr. Bill Thomas*. Retrieved from https://changingaging.org/elderhood/the-six-assets-of-aging

13. Niu, Siyu. "The Impact of the Digital Divide on the Mental Health of Older People." SHS Web of Conferences, February 13, 2023. https://www.shs-conferences.org/articles/shsconf/abs/2023/06/shsconf_essc2023_01010/shsconf_essc2023_01010.html

14. Smith, M., Segal, J. & White, M. The Six Assets of Aging. *Help Guide.org*. Retrieved from https://www.helpguide.org/aging/healthy-aging/staying-healthy-as-you-age

15. Stevenson, J. M. "Ageing and Health." Home/Newsroom, Fact
Sheets, Detail/Ageing and Health, 2024. https://www.who.int/
news-room/fact-sheets/detail/ageing-and-health

16. Terra Bella Senior Living. (2023, September 10th). Facing
New Environments with Grace. *Terra Bella Senior Living.*
Retrieved from https://www.terrabellaseniorliving.com/
senior-living-blog/the-importance-of-adaptability-skills-
for-seniors

17. Valenti, Joe. "Financial Access Challenges for Older Adults."
Financial Security & Retirement Planning, September 9, 2020.
https://www.aarp.org/pri/topics/work-finances-retirement/
financial-security-retirement/financial-access-challenges-for-
older-adults

CHAPTER 15: AN ENCORE

1. Attia, P. (2023). Outlive: Work in Progress: The High Price
of Ignoring Emotional Health. In *Outlive: The Science & Art
of Longevity* (pp. 291-306, 311-316, 322--330). New York:
Penguin Random House.

2. Applewhite, A. (2000). *This Chair Rocks: A Manifesto Against
Ageism.* New York: Celadon Books.

3. Burnight, Kerry. "Part I: What Is Joyspan?" Essay. In *Joyspan:
The Art and Science of Thriving in Life's Second Half,* First-ed.,
3–72. New York, New York: Worthy Publishers, 2025.

4. Chittister, Joan. "Fulfillment." Essay. In *The Gift of Years:
Growing Old Gracefully* 1, First-ed., 1:55–64. New York, New
York: Blue Ridge, 2008.

5. Gendron, Tracey. *Ageism unmasked: Exploring age bias and how to end it.* Lebanon, NH: Steerforth Press, 2022.

6. Gillman. "Charlotte Perkins Gilman." Charlotte Perkins Gilman, August 13, 2025. https://www.britannica.com/biography/Charlotte-Perkins-Gilman

7. Hollis, James. "Chapter 1: Expensive Ghosts: How Did We Get to This Point." Essay. In *Finding Meaning in the Second Half of Life: How to Finally Grow Up*, 1st ed., 1:1729. 1. New York, New York : Avery: Inprint of Penguin Random House, 2005.

8. Leider, Richard. "The Power of Purpose." Blue Zones, March 3, 2024. https://www.bluezones.com/2015/12/the-power-of-purpose-9-questions-for-richard-leider

9. Levy, B. (2022). *Breaking the Code: How Your Beliefs About Aging Determine How Long & Well You Live.* New York: Harper Collins.

10. McHugh, Caroline. "The Art of Being Yourself." *Ted Talk.* Lecture, April 3, 2024.

11. Piper, Mary. "Travel Skills Section 2." Essay. In *Women Rowing North: Navigating Life's Current and Flourishing as We Age*, 1, 1st ed., 1:98–160. 1. New York, New York: Bloomsbury, 2019.

12. Pressfield, Steven. "Section 85-Section 91." Essay. In *The War of Art: Break Through the Blocks and Win Your Inner Creative Battles* 1, 1st ed., 1:125–44. 1. New York, New York: Black Irish Entertainment, 2002.

13. Schachter-Shalomi, Zalman, and Ronald S. Miller. *From age-ing to sage-ing: A profound new vision of growing older.* New York: Grand Central Publishing, 2014.

14. Smith, Emily Esfahani. "There's More to Life than Being Happy (TED Talk)." May 4, 2024.

15. Waldinger, Robert. "What Makes A Good Life (TED Talk)." May 5, 2024.

16. Wattier, Linda. "3 Enablers of Purposeful Living After 60." *Sixty+Me*, April 14, 2025. https://sixtyandme.com/enablers-purposeful-living

GLOSSARY ENDNOTES

1. Applewhite, Ashton. 2019. *This Chair Rocks: A Manifesto against Ageism*. New York, NY.

2. Attia, Peter. 2023. *Outlive: The Science & Art of Longevity* New York, New York: Penguin Random House USA New York: Macmillan Audio.

3. Burnight, Kerry. 2025. "Part I: Why You're Joyspan Matters." Essay. In *Joyspan: The Art and Science of Thriving in Life's Second Half*, 1st ed., 1:3–71. 1. New York, New York: Worthy Publishers.

4. Burnight, Kerry. 2025. *Joyspan: The Art and Science of Thriving in Life's Second Half*. Nashville, Tennessee: Worthy Publishing.

5. Friedan, Betty. 2021. "Betty Friedan Quotes." *Brainy Quote*. Brainy Quote. https://www.brainyquote.com/quotes/betty_friedan_383994

6. Friedman, Marc. 2007. "The Encore Years." *The New York Times*, January 20.

7. Gendron, Tracey. 2022. *Ageism Unmasked: Exploring Age Bias and How to End It*. Lebanon, NH: Steerforth Press.

8. Kabat-Zinn, Jon, dir. 2016. *What Is Mindfulness?* Mindfulness 360. https://www.youtube.com/watch?v=0BWC9kZevxU.

9. Leardi, Jeanette. 2024. "Age and the Potential to Change." Web log. *Changing Aging with Dr. Bill Thomas.* hYps://changingaging. org/elderhood/the-six-assets-of-aging

10. Levy, Becca. 2022. *Breaking the Age Code: How Your Beliefs about Aging Determine How Long & Well You Live.* New York, NY, New York: William Morrow, an imprint of HarperCollins Publishers.

11. McLeod, Julianna. 2024. "Stress Relief: Mindfulness Techniques for Seniors and Caregivers." *All Seniors Care Centers.* All Seniors Care Centers. February 23. https://allseniorscare.com/stress-relief-mindfulness-techniques-for-seniors-and-caregivers

12. Narnia, Rachel. 2023. "The #1 Reason to Pick Up an Instrument after 50." *AARP.* November 23. https://www.aarp.org/health/brain-health/info-2023/brain-health-benefits-of-learning-an-instrument.html

13. Wong, Leung C, W. W. Li, Y Cao, and D H Shum. 2022. "The Application of Technology to Improve Cognition in Older Adults: A Review and Suggestions for Future Directions." *National Library of Medicine.* National Center for Biotechnology. June 8. https://pubmed.ncbi.nlm.nih.gov/35675967

INDEX

ABOUT THE AUTHOR

Richard A. Giaquinto is a writer, educator, and lifelong New Yorker who believes that later life can bring about quiet revelations. Much of his writing is inspired by the soft light of the Stephen A. Schwarzman Library, where the familiar faces of the staff, the silence of the reading rooms, and the steady pulse of the city outside remind him daily of the importance of storytelling. Richard's journey to the encore years has been shaped by the people who have supported him through every chapter of his life: his wife, Selvi, whose love steadies his days; his sister, JoAnn, who is always there for him; his daughters, Dita and Dyah, who continue to inspire him with their courage and creativity; his wonderful extended family, the Natawidjajas; and the friends, librarians, and coaches who fill his life with encouragement, humor, and grace. Their presence has taught him that purpose is found not in grand gestures but in small acts of connection and kindness.

As a lifelong educator and musician, Richard approaches aging with the belief that every season of life offers new opportunities to grow, heal, and rediscover joy. He lives in New York City, where he continues to observe, reflect, and write about the extraordinary richness of everyday life. *The Encore Years: Reclaiming Purpose and Visibility in Your Third Act* is his second book.